A CHICAGO TAVERN

A Goat, a Curse, and the American Dream

First Edition

By
RICK KOGAN

LAKE CLAREMONT PRESS
www.lakeclaremont.com

A Chicago Tavern: a Goat, a Curse, and the American Dream
by Rick Kogan

Published August 2006 by:
lcp@lakeclaremont.com
www.lakeclaremont.com

All photos courtesy of the Sianis family, except the contemporary photo on
the cover, by George Motz, and the photos on pages 79, 103 (bottom), 104
(bottom), and 118, by Charles Osgood.

Publisher's Cataloging-In-Publication Data
(*Prepared by The Donohue Group, Inc.*)

Kogan, Rick.

A Chicago tavern : a goat, a curse, and the American dream / Rick Kogan.
— 1st ed.

p. : ill. ; cm.

ISBN: 1-893121-49-6

1. Billy Goat Tavern (Chicago, Ill.) 2. Bars (Drinking establishments)—
Illinois—Chicago—History. 3. Sianis, William. 4. Sianis, Sam. 5. Chicago
(Ill.)—History—20th century. 6. Chicago Cubs (Baseball team)—History—
20th century . 7. Greek Americans—Illinois—Chicago—Biography. I. Title.

F548.625 K64 2006
977.3042   2006924510

10 09 08 07 06   10 9 8 7 6 5 4 3 2 1

Printed in the United States of America by United Graphics, Inc., of Mattoon,
Illinois.

for Fiona

There is no good reason to be sitting in a tavern long after last call but that's where I am right now and the clock on the wall behind the bar is flirting with 3 A.M.

Like all tavern clocks, this one is 20 minutes fast, but at least it is moving, or seems to be. Another clock on the far wall has been stuck at six for as long as I can remember, though for all I can remember right now the clock went up yesterday.

I am in the Billy Goat Tavern, a subterranean saloon underneath Michigan Avenue and a short walk from the Chicago River. This is a lonely, empty time, these hours between last call and sunrise. I see the late customers leave, unsteady up the stairs and on their way to what I know will be uneasy dreams. But now there is cash to count, ashtrays to empty, a grill to shut down, chairs to be placed upside down on tables, and a floor to sweep, and that is why Sam Sianis is still here. He owns the place.

It is quiet, or so it seems. A tavern is never as quiet as it seems. It is filled with echoes and memories, of conversations and laughter, of faces and fights, and here there are 40 years' worth hanging heavy in the stale air and making time matter not at all. And so, as Sam sits down across the table and says, "It snows maybe later. You want something to drink?" it is easy for me to see him across the room.

It is long ago and he is as young as spring and as strong as a bull. He is wearing a white shirt and a black bow tie. He is leaning over. He is biting down on the leg of a barstool. His hands are behind his back. He stands and the stool rises with him, in his teeth, into the smoke-choked tavern air. There are customers at tables and along the bar. Their faces are familiar but it is hard to remember names. Some are so drunk that getting off their barstools without falling down would be an impressive physical feat. But they are not moving, except to turn their heads toward Sam and to bang their bottles and glasses on the tables and on the bar.

The chair is up and Sam's face is turning red. Veins are bulging in his neck; they start to look like small ropes. Conversations stop. Someone relatively sober yells, "Go Sammy," and someone smashed says, "Sameeslikanoxsh," and others begin to shout until the whole room vibrates. After a minute that could be an hour, Sam pulls the chair from his teeth. He smacks it down hard on the floor. The room erupts in a hurtful noise. A glass shatters. Sam reaches for a rag. He moves toward the spill.

"It is late and you are still here," he says sitting across from me at the table. And, as if he has just seen what I've seen, he says, "I was very strong when I was young." Now I see tired in his shoulders and in his eyes and I ask him why he isn't home. Why don't you leave this work for your employees or your kids? You are one of the most famous tavern keepers in the world. What the hell are you doing dumping ashtrays into a trash bin? Why are you lifting chairs onto tables? Mopping the floor? While I am saying this, I get up and grab a chair.

"No, no. What are you doing? Sit down," Sam says, so firmly that if I hadn't known him all these years I would think he was mad at me. Maybe he is, but he says, "Don't worry. This is what I do. I cannot not do this. To be a manager you have to graduate from a big college. I didn't. I graduate from mopping the floors and all that. You need to clean the tables, you jump on the tables. You need to help at the bar, you jump on the bar. You see work that needs to be done, you take care of that work. That is what I learn when I come here. That is what my uncle, he teaches me, and I do it."

There is an old oil portrait of Sam's uncle on the crowded walls of the tavern. It is the largest and among the oddest of the hundreds of images that fill the walls. I have seen it a thousand times, but now Sam is telling me to look at it again

Bill Sianis with some of his more attractive customers.

as he says, "Many years ago I go to Greece and I visit the grave of my uncle. I go to his grave and I plant some bushes, and then I take a bucket and I water the bushes. Then after I come back here, I fall asleep on the couch that used to be in the office, and my uncle, he come to me and he says in Greek, 'You put all that water on top of me. You are trying to drown me.' He is joking that time, but I see him many times, in my dreams and in my life. He is very happy, never disappointed at the way I do things, how I keep his name up, his memory alive. I tell him, 'You up there, I'm down here but we both still work for the Billy Goat.' Now, you look at the picture. See? That is why he is still smiling."

A lively night during the tavern's early years.

Before he would be known as Billy Goat, Sam's uncle William Sianis lives and works in the nightmarish neighborhood that is the Union Stockyards, where the air is filled with the stench of rotting meat, burning hides, and manure-filled pens. Novelist Upton Sinclair writes about it in his 1906 novel *The Jungle*, describing its "elemental odor, raw and crude; it was rich, almost rancid, sensual, and strong." Even on sunny days, the sky darkens with the smoke of half a dozen huge chimneys and is filled with the sound, also courtesy of Sinclair, of "endless activity . . . the rumblings of a world in motion. It was the distant lowing of ten thousand cattle, the distant grunting of ten thousand swine."

There is another sound, too, the jabber of more than 40,000 workers from more than two dozen countries. Immigrants and sons of immigrants, they do hard and harsh and horrible work for low wages. Their American Dreams are washing away in the strain of the certain kind of hell that is the Stockyards and they wash away their regrets at the dozens of forlorn taverns that dot the area.

Sianis arrives with his older brother Frank at Union Station on the afternoon of January 4, 1912. He has five dollars in his shoe and his own cloudy version of the American Dream in his head. He comes from Paleopyrgos in Greece, docking in New York City on New Year's Day. In Greece he wants to study agriculture, but his father George doesn't have money for a formal education. He borrows $25 from his father, lying to him, telling him he is going to use it to visit an uncle in Athens. He borrows five dollars more from a cousin and books passage to America. After 55 days and nights at sea, and lost and confused in New York, he and Frank hop a freight train to Chicago. Frank has been to America before. In 1903 he and his father go to San Francisco but return to Greece after the earthquake and fire level the city in 1906.

They speak only a few words of English, and so all William can muster is "You help?" to a young redcap, who says, spotting an easy mark, "You have any money, any money?"

William fishes the five dollars from his shoe.

"Good," says the redcap, pocketing the bill with one hand and pointing to a door with the other. "Now go out that way and good luck to you."

The brothers walk out into the strange city. They are alone, lost, broke. They are 16 and 19, and you must right now be shuddering as you try to imagine what they go through — *What do they eat? Where do they sleep? Who do they meet?* — before getting jobs shining shoes and selling newspapers at 47th and Halsted Streets. It's a hard racket with a tough crowd. There are more than 1,000 newsboys working just for the *Tribune*; all are instructed to "scream a little louder and run a little faster alongside passing streetcars." The city has nine daily newspapers and competition is fierce. Newspaper bundles are stolen and newsboys roughed up.

The brothers become friendly with a Greek tavern owner and William says that on his "first Thanksgiving in America, that Greek fed me turkey and spaghetti in the back room of his saloon."

The newest Billy Goat Tavern opens in Washington, D.C., on a late September afternoon in 2005. Semi-dignitaries, Capitol Hill minions, and curiosity-seekers are there for the formal ribbon-cutting, at which Illinois Senator Dick Durbin says, "This is a proud day for Chicago and a great day for Washington . . . An historic day."

The walls of this new place are glass, which will not allow for the presentation of the sort of memorabilia that is so educational for those who visit the Billy Goats in Chicago. There are now seven of them: the oldest on Hubbard Street; on Navy Pier; in a terminal at O'Hare International Airport; at 309 W. Washington Street; 330 S. Wells Street; in the Merchandise Mart; and at 1535 W. Madison Street.

On the wall above the bar in the Hubbard Street Billy Goat is a stuffed goat head. This makes a lovely photo opportunity for tourists, a visual reminder of the most famous curse in sports, born in 1945 when William Sianis and a goat are not allowed to enter Wrigley Field.

Less obvious, but equally important, are the hundreds of photos on the walls, a gallery that reaches back to the 1930s and features such celebrities as Bill Veeck, Kirk Douglas, a few Chicago mayors, Hubert Humphrey, and a couple of U.S. Presidents. Dozens of the photos are of Williams Sianis, posing through the years with a number of pretty women; a variety of animals, including many goats, some fish, a duck, an elephant; with soldiers and cops; in formal settings and behind the bar.

Also on the walls are letters, framed clippings from old newspapers, and a number of signs: the self-explanatory, but absolutely false for the tavern's regulars, "WE DO NOT CASH CHECKS. NOT EVEN MY OWN . . . BILLY GOAT" and, more mysteriously, "Calvert Whiskey is <u>not</u> sold here," born of a long ago dispute with a liquor distributor.

In Washington the only hints of history are found on two plasma-screen TVs on either side of a fake marble bar. On the sets are tapes of *Saturday Night Live* skits more than two decades old. There is John Belushi, Bill Murray, Dan Aykroyd — *so young* — and a variety of guest hosts doing their network TV best to recreate the not yet famous "Cheezborger, cheezborger! No fries . . . chips!" mantra of the Billy Goat. These clips, still funny after all these years, are accompanied by dozens of other clips from TV news broadcasts that tell the story of the curse, again and again and again.

Still, a number of people look confused and can be seen scratching their heads when Senator Durbin refers to the Billy Goat as a "national institution."

William Sianis is tough and enterprising. While his brother Frank continues to make a living shining shoes, William is soon selling papers on three corners around the stockyards, supplementing his income by selling light bulbs that he steals from trolley cars and by cadging streetcar transfers from people coming to work and then selling them to those on their way home.

"At first I don't know how to do this, and the police they gave me a very hard time. Told me I would be arrested. But then I came up with an idea. I put the transfers in the papers and I would say, 'page 4' or 'page 6,' so the people would know where to find the transfer," he says.

He falls in love with newspapers and the men who write for them. He learns English by reading the papers and the bylines above the stories; the names of the writers become as important, as dear, to him as if they were real people, older brothers almost, taking him by the hand to baseball games, crime scenes, society parties, or fancy night clubs and restaurants.

In 1916, he becomes an American citizen and later works for a time as a copy boy for the *Tribune*. By 1926 he has enough money to buy a small building near the lake on what is then a bleak and empty stretch of Illinois Street. He lives upstairs and on the ground level opens a small restaurant that struggles to survive for a few years before being done in shortly after the 1929 stock-market crash. He sells the building, shuts the restaurant, and returns to where he came from, opening a newsstand at 47th and Halsted Streets, where he sells not only newspapers but also cigars, candy, and magazines.

He sells the December 6, 1933, editions that announce the end of Prohibition, and within two months he is behind the bar of a shot-and-beer joint called the Lincoln Tavern, a former speakeasy at 1855 W. Madison Street across the street from the new Chicago Stadium. There are few people alive who can recall with any accuracy or reliability the way it looks, which is in the style of the classic Chicago neighborhood tavern: a long bar fronting one wall of the rectangular space, tables filling the floor, and a few booths on the opposite wall, with a small dance floor near the back.

Like many of the stories that surround the Billy Goat, the tale of how Sianis comes to own this tavern and its three-story building is massaged into myth by imaginative reporters, told and retold like this: Sianis plunks down two $100 personal checks and a $5 bill as down payment on the property, and when the checks bounce three days later, convinces the building's owner to carry him until he can pay it off.

The real story is this: "My uncle, he does not have enough money to buy any place," says Sam. "But he is able to borrow $500 from a businessman he know. That's what he use to buy the Lincoln Tavern, and, after a while, when he save the money to pay the man back, he goes to his house and a lady answers the door. She ask what he wants and he tells her that he is there to pay the man back the $500. She tells him that she is the man's wife and that the man has passed away. He tries to give her the money but she says, 'No.' She tells my uncle, 'Keep the money for good luck.'"

Paddy Harmon is a former newsboy and one of the city's leading sports promoters. He wants to buy a

National Hockey League franchise for Chicago, but unable to make that deal, decides instead to own the building in which the team will play. The Chicago Stadium, with 25,000 seats, is the largest indoor arena in the world, built with $2.5 million of Harmon's own money and $7 million he borrows from friends.

It opens on March 17, 1929, with a prizefight, and the Blackhawks play their first hockey game there that December 16. Within a year, Harmon is dead, killed in a car crash in the suburbs. He is 53 and dies with three dollars in his pocket and to his name. His last wish is to be "laid out" at the Stadium, and the arena is draped in black and purple as hundreds of people pays their respects.

All sorts of unusual events take place in the Stadium. On December 18, 1932, with the Chicago Bears' Wrigley Field home iced over, the team plays indoors against the Portland Spartans for the league championship. In front of 11,198 people, Bronko Nagurski passes two yards to Red Grange for the only touchdown scored on a shortened 80-yard field. One kickoff almost sails through a Stadium window.

But the place struggles through the early years of the Depression until real estate developer Arthur Wirtz gains control of it in 1934. He signs the darling of the 1932 Winter Olympics in Lake Placid, blond ice queen Sonja Henie, to a series of tremendously successful ice shows that fill the Stadium's seats.

One morning in the early summer of 1934, a baby goat falls off a truck traveling east on Madison Street. Dazed and limping, it wanders into the Lincoln Tavern. Sianis sees the goat and sends one of his waiters out to get a baby bottle. While he is feeding the goat, a lawyer sitting at the bar suggests that Sianis adopt the goat, saying, "You'll get a million dollars worth of free publicity." This seems like a very good idea to Sianis since his cash register is taking in only seven dollars a day. David Condon, a *Tribune* columnist who becomes one of the most prolific and imaginative chroniclers of Sianis' activities, writes that the tavern owner went to court where "the attorney and judge conferred. The judge paroled the goat 'into the custody of William Sianis for life.'"

Immediately, Sianis renames his tavern the Billy Goat Inn and begins to grow a spade goatee to fit the part. There is a small patch of grass in the yard in back of the tavern, and there the goat lives and happily nibbles, the first of many goats to call the place home. "All of the Chicago police, if they find a stray goat, and a long time ago there were lots of goats wandering around, they bring them to my uncle," says Sam. "They know that my uncle will take good care of the goats."

The first time the Billy Goat appears in print is on June 19, 1938, in the *Tribune*: "One great personality in Our Town is a goat." It isn't much, just a couple of paragraphs, the first item in a column called "Our Town." It tells of the tavern and details Billy's trouble getting a copy of his U.S. citizenship papers because the photo he sent to Washington no longer resembles the 22-year-old, whiskerless picture that has been on file since 1916. "Billy could solve it right away with a shave, but he just can't bring himself to do it," the anonymous columnist writes.

That the columnist has no byline is not unusual. That's the way it is in these days, when bylines have to be earned, sometimes over years of writing stories. But the writer is well-acquainted with Billy and his tavern. That's the way it is in these days, too. Newspapers and booze have been joined at the hip for at least a couple of centuries, and few places ever provided as comforting a home for the press as the Billy Goat.

Billy installs a battery of phones in the back of the tavern so reporters can call in their stories about the events they cover at the Stadium. Photographers, lugging their big Flash cameras, drop in between assignments. There is plenty to shoot, as the Stadium hosts an ever-widening array of ice shows, circuses, rodeos, boxing matches; religious, civic and labor gatherings; and political conventions.

On the first day of the 1944 Republican National Convention, Billy is disappointed to have done only $20 in business. That night he puts a hand-made sign in the window: "No Republicans Served Here." Word spreads quickly across the convention floor and soon dozens of angry delegates, most of them wearing buttons touting the eventual nominee, Thomas Dewey, pack the tavern and demand to be served. When they stumble from the bar and back to the arena, they proudly announce, "I guess we showed that Democratic son of a bitch! Go over there and make him serve you a drink." Meanwhile, Billy is on the phone: "Send over five more barrels of beer. Business has never been better." That day he takes in $2,600.

Between Stadium events, Billy proves a masterful and cagey showman, his place becoming what one reporter refers to as a "perpetual Halloween."

"The trick I think is that he treat everybody the same," says Sam. "The very first thing he tells me is, 'You are responsible to everyone, you like them, and don't try to cheat them. Give the people what they want, and try to be good friends and be a sport.'"

When *The New Yorker* magazine writer and tavern enthusiast, A.J. Liebling, comes to the city in the 1940s, he observes, in a 1951 article that gives Chicago its "Second City" nickname, and a book entitled *Chicago: The Second City*, that "A thing about Chicago that impressed me from the hour I got there was the saloons. New York bars operate on the principle that you want a drink or you wouldn't be there. If you are civil and don't mind waiting, they will sell you one when they get around to it. Chicago bars assume that nobody likes liquor, and that to induce the customers to purchase even a minute quantity, they have to provide a show."

Liebling never mentions the Billy Goat. But an ardent boxing fan and arguably the sport's most poetic reporter, it's likely that before or after one of the many prizefights held at the Chicago Stadium, he visits the antic tavern across the street.

"Provide a show": that is the philosophy that guides Billy. He gives his customers swing bands like Scotty and His Royal Michiganders, B-girls, beer drinking and dollar-bill-eating goats, a duck named Susie Q, a one-toothed cat named Ruby, an endless series of practical jokes and funny stories, fire gongs clanging and police sirens screeching for crowds that usually includes his three favorite types of customers — politicians, policemen, and newspaper reporters — in addition to members of whatever shows are at the Stadium: circus clowns, ice skaters, cowboys, bearded ladies, tattooed men, hockey players, midgets . . . and their fans.

There are no silly laws insisting that taverns close at a specific hour, and so there are no clocks at all in the Billy Goat, and there are days in a row that it never closes so anybody can at any hour experience what one reporter affectionately describes as "a unique establishment that combines the salient eccentricities of a police station, a fire house, a street carnival, and a menagerie, and then some."

Ray Sons covers the Blackhawks for the *Daily News* in the early 1960s and remembers, "The tavern was the place to buy hockey tickets at Billy's inflated prices, when every Hawk game was a sellout. This was in the seasons when Bobby Hull, Stan Mikita, Glenn Hall, and Pierre Pilote were sufficiently entertaining they could have sold thousands more tickets for every game. I don't know how Billy got his plentiful supply, but there certainly had to be more than friendship with the Stadium ticket sellers."

"It is," Sam says, "a fun place."

Sam is born in the tiny Greek village of Paleopyrgos early on the morning of December 12, 1935. His mother is named Theofana. "But I never get to know her. She dies one hour after I am born," he says. He is fed goat milk as an infant and is raised by his father, Anthanasios, who will have four other children, three boys and a girl, from two other marriages, and by a large extended family, which includes his grandmothers and a number of aunts and uncles.

"I was only little boy when my uncle Billy Goat comes back to the village. Everyone is very excited to see him and to hear his stories. He has this little beard, a goatee, and he was very nice to me," Sam says.

17

It helps his memory that he has photos from that visit taped to the wall of his office, a spectacularly cramped and messy little room tucked behind the grill at the Billy Goat. One of them shows his uncle, a sturdy man with dark eyes and a dark goatee, standing on a mountainside with a rifle over his shoulder. Another photo, which makes Sam laugh every time he shows it to the very few people he will allow in the office, is of himself at the time, three years old and naked from the waist down.

"I leave school after only one year of high school," says Sam. "I work on the farm all the time. I do everything . . . plow with horses, cut wheat. There were no machines. We do everything by hand. This makes me strong."

He is 19 when he travels by boat to America, arriving in New York on May 15, 1955. A three day train trip later he is in San Francisco where he joins his aunts Margo and Pat, who still live there, and helps in the coffee shop they own. He washes dishes, mops floors, and waits tables. He is paid $30 a week. He lives in his aunts' house and enjoys the company of the diner's customers, most of them Greek and many of them working for the railroads. Within a year they help get Sam a job as an apprentice mechanic for the Southern Pacific Railroad. "Sure, I like the work," he says. "But then because the airplanes start to become very popular, the trains they don't do so well. I was laid off after four years."

On July 4, 1960, he arrives in Chicago to work at the Billy Goat Inn.

"It is a nice place the first time I see it. There is a hotel on the corner and a coffee shop next door," Sam says. "I get to live upstairs, sharing the apartment with my uncle and he puts me to work right away. I am mopping the floors, filling the coolers, cleaning tables, tending the bar, and feeding the goats that live out in the back. There are lots of goats, but the famous goat that makes the curse, she is not alive any more."

Before the fourth game of the World Series between the Chicago Cubs and the Detroit Tigers at Wrigley Field on October 6, 1945, a special bus carrying reporters from their headquarters at the Palmer House breaks down at Belmont Avenue, forcing the newsmen to thumb rides to the park; actress June Haver rushes onto the field and kisses Cubs' manager Charlie Grimm; team owner Philip K. Wrigley entertains National League executives in the club's private press lounge called the Pink Poodle; Andy Frain has 525 ushers on hand to handle the crowd of 42,923. Only one of those people is causing a problem.

Billy arrives at the field with two tickets and one of his goats, Murphy, who is wearing a blanket with a sign pinned to it: "We Got Detroit's Goat." They have tickets, seats 6 and 7, box 65, tier 12, which cost $7.20 each — but they are stopped at the gate.

Billy asks the ushers to ask Mr. Wrigley if he and his goat can enter the park. Up in the Pink Poodle, Wrigley says that he is happy for Billy to come in and watch the game "but the goat stays out because he smells."

Billy is used to taking goats places. Since many Stadium employees are frequent Billy Goat guests, they allow Billy and his goat into events. *Who'd notice a goat during circuses, rodeos, and hockey games?* Billy is ingenious about getting a goat into political conventions; once he hides the creature in a satchel labeled "ABC." He gets a goat into the hospital room to see one of his reporter friends. And Ruby is such a frequent Stadium visitor that the one-toothed cat has, the newspapers dutifully report, a "favorite perch in the rafters."

But at Wrigley Field, Billy and his goat are denied entrance and return to the tavern where newspaper photographers want Billy, in protest and as a photo opportunity, to feed the goat the unused ticket. "No. I keep it for evidence," he says. "I am going to sue for $100,000 — no, I sue for a million!"

Billy tells his story to reporters and quickly it gets back to the papers. First, Arch Ward in the *Tribune* and a couple of days later *Sun* columnist Irv Kupcinet write playful items about Billy's outrage. There is no mention of a curse or a hex or a jinx.

Detroit wins the fifth game, also played in Chicago, 8–4. The Cubs win the sixth game in Detroit, 8–7, in the bottom of the 12th inning. The seventh game in Chicago is no contest. The Tigers score five runs in the first inning and win 9–3. Billy sends a telegram to Wrigley.

It reads, tersely, "Who stinks now?"

On May 15, 1953, the Stadium hosts the second Rocky Marciano-Joe Walcott heavyweight-title bout. Walcott checks out in the fist round, and many in the crowd, with unexpected free time on their hands, make their way to the Billy Goat.

The place is packed when Frank Sinatra, Joe DiMaggio, and Leo Durocher walk in together. There is no place to sit. It is hard to move. Billy offers the celebrity trio a deal: They can use Billy's private phone booth and he will personally deliver drinks to them. When he does, Sinatra hands Billy a $20. Sinatra asks for change and Billy tells him there isn't any, saying, "The prices, they are higher in the phone booth." Sinatra, who is not a man to be messed with when and where alcohol is involved, just laughs. Billy asks him to pose for a picture.

By this time, the tavern's walls are filled with the photos of many famous people, but Billy has an amazing facility for remembering everybody's face, a talent he displays on a lazy

1955 afternoon when a dignified-looking man walks into the bar and asks for a brandy. Billy pours it and the man hands him a $5 bill.

"I know you," says Billy. "You were a redcap?"

"That's a long time ago," says the man. "I am a doctor now, but yes, when I was going to medical school, I did work as a redcap at Union Station."

Billy puts the $5 bill in his pocket.

"Hey, what's going on?" says the doctor. "No change?"

"You don't remember me, do you?" says Billy.

"No, sorry, I don't," he says.

"Just trust me. You owe me this five dollars from a very long time ago," says Billy. "The brandy, don't worry. It's on the house."

Thanks to the Cubs' continuing ineptitude, Billy's press pals start to joke with him, saying that he must have put a curse or hex on the team. Billy plays along.

Late in the 1950 season, *Sun-Times* sports' editor Gene Kessler suggests Billy write a letter saying that he will remove the curse in exchange for a formal apology. Kessler prints Billy's letter and Wrigley's response: "Will you please extend to [your goat] my sincere apologies . . . and ask him not only to remove the 'hex' but to reverse the flow and start pulling for wins."

A Chicago Tavern

The Cubs keep on losing, but in July 1959, with the White Sox leading the American League, Billy spots team owner, friend, and frequent tavern-patron Bill Veeck at Comiskey Park. He takes out a blank check and hands it to Veeck, saying "That's for my World Series tickets."

Veeck hands the check back to Billy, saying, "This is too early. Don't jinx us."

The Sox make the series that year, and one night at the bar Billy buys two tickets from Veeck. "We know where those seats are," says Veeck. "The cops will check. Don't bring in your goat. The World Series is not for goats."

Billy exchanges his tickets for a pair in another location and gets a goat into the park. But Veeck has them tossed out. The next day, Billy tells Condon, "Veeck said I'd never get the goat in again. But I paid $150 to a helicopter to drop me and my goat at second base just before the seventh game." That game never comes: The Sox lose the Series to the Los Angeles Dodgers out in L.A.

The next year, *Sun-Times* sports columnist, Jerome Holtzman, promotes the candidacy of a goat named Billy V for the job of Cubs' manager. "He has been boning up on baseball," Billy tells Holtzman, adding that the goat eats sports pages every day and has also devoured a dozen *Baseball Guides*. "Sianis says that Billy V is willing to let bygones be bygones. His pet will remove the ancestral hex," writes Holtzman.

A Chicago Tavern

If you do not know him—or even if you are a great admirer, a colleague, or a close friend—it is not always a good idea to approach Mike Royko when he is sitting alone on a stool in the Billy Goat. That's where he is now, and a young man across the bar has had too much to drink and is shouting at Royko, "Big man . . . Big shot columnist." He offers to buy Mike a drink. Mike says, "No thanks." The young man approaches and I get off my stool and stand between the man and Mike because if I get in a barroom fight no one will care. If Mike does, it makes headlines.

"You too big a man to give my uncle an autograph?" says the guy.

"If it'll shut you up," Mike says. "What's your uncle's name?"

The young man, obviously surprised, says, "His name, his name is Henry."

Mike asks the bartender for one of the paper bags that sit in a stack behind the bar. He lays the bag flat on the bar and with a pen writes something. I lean over his shoulder and see, "Dear Uncle Henry, your nephew is an a———. Sincerely, Mike Royko."

Mike hands the bag to the kid who reads it aloud and then says "Oh, man. Thanks, thanks so much, Mr. Royko. He'll love this. My uncle will love this. Thanks. Just thanks." He presses the bag to his chest as Mike says, "You're welcome, lad, now move along," and returns to his drink.

A
GOAT

A customer delights in a goat's beer-drinking ability.

Billy Sianis, in one of the few suits he owned, strikes a relatively formal pose with the goat that started it all.

More distinguished with age, Billy draws a beer.

Billy and some human pals pose with one of the goats.

A fire at a nearby building allowed for one of the few photos ever taken of the exterior of the tavern on Madison Street.

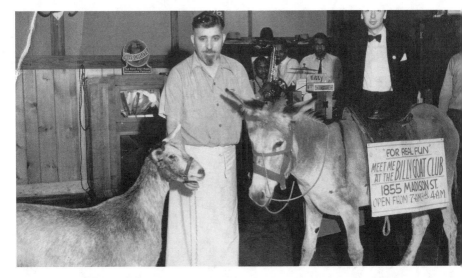

It wasn't just goats that called the tavern home. In the background is house band Scotty and His Royal Michiganders.

A wake for one of the tavern's denizens.

Billy's portrait was the most prominent on the Wall of Fame.

Sam behind the bar at Hubbard Street, serving a "pal."

A Chicago Tavern

Mike is not the first journalist to use the Billy Goat as an oasis, and, occasionally, a stage. But no writer is more closely associated with the Billy Goat and none more colorfully epitomizes the hard-drinking image of the Chicago newspaperman.

Only Billy Goat himself has more pictures on the walls of the tavern than Mike. Many go up during the years that Mike is writing, but after he dies in 1997, the place becomes as close to a shrine as any newspaperman has ever had. Mike's face, his columns, the obituary from the *Tribune*, and stories about him catch your eye no matter in which direction you are looking.

"I miss Mike very much," Sam tells me in the early Sunday morning of May 7, 2000. I remember the day because it is the first time Sam ever tells me that he sees ghosts. "I see Mike three, four times. Matter of fact, I see him three days ago. Mike come by here. It was when he was dead. I ask him if he remembers when I said, 'Mike, if anything ever happen to me, I want you to keep the Billy Goat name alive.' And he nods his head and I tell him, 'Now that you are gone I am going to keep your name alive. I'm going to make sure your name will live forever.'"

Sam still sees Mike. He sees him sitting on the stool he usually occupied in what is known as "Wise Guy's Corner," the section along the bar just to the right of the stairway.

A Chicago Tavern

"He was more than best friend. He was better than a brother," Sam says. "We meet the first time a few days after the new Billy Goat open on Hubbard Street. Mike was at a table with my uncle, and they were talking and laughing. I was working at the grill."

Mike is a tavern kid. He calls himself a "flat-above-a-tavern youth" because he grows up in the apartment above the tavern his parents own, the Blue Sky Lounge. He is comfortable there and in all taverns afterward, and he writes about them often. In the introduction to my book called *Dr. Night Life's Chicago* he writes, "I believe that getting a drink should be a simple matter. You walked from your home to the corner bar which was usually stocked with all a reasonable person needed: shots, beers, hardboiled eggs, dried beef, potato chips, a juke box, a pin ball machine . . . It might also provide some recreational activities: a softball team, a bookie and, on Friday and Saturday nights, a two piece band (accordion and drums)."

Figuring that "any goof could write a newspaper story," he works for a community newspaper and the City New Bureau. He is hired by the *Daily News* in 1959, working first on the day shift before moving to nights. During the days, he sells tombstones over the phone and through home visits to supplement his income. He starts as a full-time columnist in January 1964. The Billy Goat opens on Hubbard Street three months later, on March 4, the birthday of the city of Chicago.

"Mike come down, especially on Sunday, and a lot of times he calls first and say, 'What are you doing?' and I would say 'I'm down here,' and he says, 'If you don't got anything to do this afternoon, let's go to the Bears' game.' The Bears play in Wrigley Field then, but even when the Bears move to Soldier Field, we still would go."

Whenever he talks about Mike, Sam's voice lowers and his eyes well with tears. "A lot of laughs with Mike here," he says. "A lot of laughs we had . . . "

The tavern on Madison Street closes in October 1964. Condon suggests two reasons for this: "Chicago got this silly thing about closing saloons at 4 A.M . . . Fewer sport events and political conventions came to be held at the Stadium. So the death of Madison Street's most famous oasis was inevitable." There is another reason: The neighborhood around the Stadium is deteriorating and getting increasingly dangerous with shootings, stabbings, and muggings taking place after almost every Stadium event.

By this time, the new place has been open for seven months in what was a quick-to-fail Chinese restaurant on Hubbard Street in the basement of the year-old Apollo Savings & Loan building. This gives the new Billy Goat Tavern a classy formal address, 430 N. Michigan Avenue, though the tavern is in the process of becoming a cave within a cave as construction begins on an upper level off Michigan Avenue, creating what is called the Plaza of the Americas. It will contain 35 flags, a patch of greenery, a huge statue of Benito Juarez, and will forever hide the Billy Goat from sunlight. Nevertheless, this location delights the employees of the four newspapers who find themselves within crawling distance of the tavern: the *Tribune* and *American,* housed in a gothic tower and its stocky sidekick on Michigan Avenue, and to the west, in a seven-story modern building on the banks of the river at Wabash Avenue and meant to resemble a boat, the *Sun-Times* and *Daily News.*

The presses that print the papers are housed in each of these buildings, providing a large pool of new customers: printers, typesetters, pressmen, stereotypers, engravers, and circulation drivers. Billy is happy about this, but not always. "Some of them, they are so covered in ink they make the place filthy," he complains, and he does not allow the printers to sit on bar stools if they have ink on their pants.

He also disapproves of another new element of downtown tavern life, the miniskirt. He discourages male patrons from staring at the legs of women and tells Mike, "I can't get used to women sitting there with that much showing. I keep expecting the vice detectives to come in and arrest me for running a house."

A Chicago Tavern

Before, and for a couple of decades after, the Billy Goat moves into its new neighborhood, there are plenty of other nearby places to satisfy a thirst.

The Radio Grill on East Illinois Street and later on Grand Avenue has been a newspaper hangout since 1935. "A newspaper desirous of a sudden late edition could call the Radio Grill and find enough help for the task at hand, and often did," writes the *Tribune*'s Paul Holmes. It is owned by Harry Grossman who, it is said, has made millions off the place because, Holmes speculates, "He never bought a drink for a customer, at least publicly, that is, and he whittled his martinis down to size by stirring ice cubes in half an ounce of gin for 10 minutes to get enough liquid to cover the olive."

But he is also the softest of soft touches when a newspaperman is in trouble, or a homeless person needs money for a meal or a coat. Bartender Frank Morgner, who owns a piece of the tavern, will tell you stories about how he lost his leg when he was nine, and how he and another kid parlayed their one-leggedness into a successful career as a tumbling and dancing team in vaudeville and the circus. He has been working at the Radio Grill since 1942, and many circus people drop in to visit. One of them brings in a trained bear who stands at the bar and drinks beer from a bowl. Frank doesn't like to serve circus midgets; they used to steal his wooden leg. But nothing gets him down: "They're not going to lick me. I'm just as good as any man with two legs. I can win, and I'm going to win."

The St. Louis Browns is in a basement on East Illinois Street, its fake brick walls filled with photographs of the lamentable St. Louis Browns baseball team and some of its distinctive players, such as one-armed outfielder Pete Gray and Eddie Gaedel, the midget sent in to pinch-hit as a stunt by then team owner Bill Veeck. The Corona Cafe, on two different corners of Rush Street, starts life as a speakeasy in 1920 and claims to be the first place in the country to serve table wines in carafes. Editors eat fat charcoal-broiled steaks washed down with bourbon in the front room and reporters and cabbies slurp soup and beer in the back or basement. The Press Club in the Sheraton Hotel, with its high-backed leather chairs and a special couch, is where the great sportswriter John Carmichael "rests" after long lunches. The Boul-Mich, found down a strip of soiled carpet just off Michigan Avenue above Grand Avenue, is where you can find "The Best and Largest Martini Served Anywhere," a couple of affable owners, Frank Friefield and Sam Beer, a lot of newspaper editors and writers, advertising types and a few radio and television sorts, and one man who, when served his gold fish bowl-sized martini says, "Jesus, a guy could drown in that," and walks out the door.

A wall-side ad touts the tavern's swanky new location.

In 1969, after a couple of rare winning seasons — since 1945, the Cubs had only four winning seasons, never finishing closer than 13 games out of first place and for 15 of those years finishing 25 or more games out — the Cubs in mid-August are 9½ games ahead of the New York Mets. At season's end, the Cubs are in second place, eight games behind the Mets. In the face of such an epic fall, the curse resurfaces.

Sam displays his strength by lifting a 100-pound sack of sugar.

"Some people say the Cubs ran out of gas," Billy tells Condon. "Some blame [manager Leo] Durocher. Some say they spent too much time singing about holy mackerel. Others say the Cubs were too busy selling underwear. Some say politics. Some say it was the Bleacher Bums. Some say it was the Billy Goat hex cost the Cubs the pennant. When the Billy Goat hex is on you, there is nothing except trouble."

Billy also tells Condon this: "I wrote a personal letter to Mr. Wrigley. And I told him the hex was gone. I put that song,

Hey! Hey! Holy Mackerel [written, as very few people know, by Chicago jazzman Johnny Frigo] on my jukebox just like Mr. Wrigley has the song on his juke box in the Wrigley Building restaurant. I wanted to make up with Mr. Wrigley personally, but never ran into him as I was always looking for him at the baseball park. I even wrote a letter to Leo Durocher saying the next time my goat comes up from the farm, we would all have lunch at the Wrigley Building restaurant. Yes, I removed the Billy Goat hex from the Cubs."

The happiest and healthiest person in Wise Guy's corner is also the one who has been here the longest. Bob Borgstrom says, "When I was a teenager we'd go to hockey games at the Stadium, and between periods we'd sneak over to the original Goat. People were always four or five deep at the bar, so when we'd called out our drinks and pass over the money nobody ever asked how old we were and that was a good thing. But boy, did that place smell. Really bad because of all the animals around."

Bob and a couple of the other white-haired Billy Goat regulars remember all of the taverns and restaurants that used to pepper the neighborhood. And he remembers the day the Billy Goat opens: "It was painted a fire engine red. It was like sitting inside a firehouse. And it was tough on Billy at first. That first year he must have gone through 25 bartenders.

All of them were stealing. That's why he used to sit in a high chair right by the stairs with that kid's hammer that squeaked and that he used to use to bang on anybody he saw staring at the girls walking down the stairs and say, 'Don't pay attention to that!' What he was really doing was watching the bartenders and the cash register."

Billy trusted Sam, but needing more help, he began to bring relatives over from Greece including Sam's father, Anthanasios, and his brothers John and Sava. They all work at the Billy Goat for a while before returning for keeps to Greece. His brother Frank, who came to Chicago with Billy decades before, dies one week after the Billy Goat opens on Hubbard Street. Bob smiles remembering Sam's father: "A wonderful guy. He didn't speak much English, but he was always smiling, handing bags of chips to the kids."

Bob has spent his working life on the river. He is the son of Albert Borgstrom, who in 1935 starts operating a 97-passenger wooden boat that takes sightseers from Navy Pier out into the lake. Four years later he moves his boat to the riverbank underneath Michigan Avenue, and Bob goes to work for him when he is 14.

The Wendella Sightseeing Boats is the company Bob owns; seven boats that cruise the river and lake, as well as take commuters between the train stations near Madison Street and the Michigan Avenue bridge. He turns 71 this year, just like Sam, and like Sam, continues to work hard even though he could let his employees, his kids do it. What the hell are you doing cleaning engines at 6 A.M.? Why aren't you at your other home in Florida, fishing or sipping cocktails with Lila, your wife of 55 years?

"I like the work," he says. "And I like this place. I remember coming in for coffee every morning about 6:30, and the place would be filled with guys in suits and ties getting ready for their day, having Bloody Marys and screwdrivers. And Sam used to bring in a 30-pound lamb at Greek Easter and feed the homeless. And Condon, sitting here with those big cigars and eating raw steak. And on Friday and Saturday nights you'd get the crews from the boats bringing the newsprint down from Canada, a wild crowd."

He pauses and sips a beer and stares around the tavern.

"All these memories, like ghosts. And I can't even remember the first time a celebrity walked in here," he says. "Doesn't matter. Like I said, I like it here."

Many years ago, Mike asks Sam a question: "What are you going to do if you win the lottery? Where would you go?"

"I'm not gonna go anyplace," Sam tells him. "Even if I go far away, it would not be the same. I'd rather be here and talk to you and see friends. If I go someplace else, I would only see strange people. My hobby? My hobby is to be down here and be with friends and talk."

Bob is in the Billy Goat two or three times a week when the boats are running, standing in Wise Guy's corner, shortly after what is a normal person's lunch hour, talking with friends.

"This is the best bar in the city," he says, and while he is saying this, Sam walks over. Even though they see each other often during the week, they greet like long-lost friends. The affection is obvious, as Bob throws his arm around Sam's shoulders and pinches his cheek.

A few minutes later he says, "Sam is like a brother to me. I've never asked him for anything, but I know I could ask him for anything, and he would never turn me down. And I'd do the same for him. If you don't love this guy then you can't love anybody."

Among Bob's many memories is that of the day in 1981 when a young man named Jeff Magill comes in to interview for a job as bartender.

"You going to work for Sam?" Bob asks.

"Don't know," says Jeff. "What do you think?"

"It'll be a good job," says Bob. "And Sam will be a good boss."

Magill takes the job. He is still here.

I have my first drink at Melvin's, where Rush Street meets State Street. It is a cold night and the outdoor patio is closed. I ask for a Jack Daniel's with one ice cube, an order so specific so as to convince the waitress that I have such vast tavern experience that there will be no need for her to ask for my ID, which would tell her that I am 16. She does not and over the next decades I have drinks in many different taverns, a few gin mills, some after-hours dives, piano bars, all-night strip clubs in Cicero, lounges, discos, and one place with the most practical tavern name in history, Stop & Drink.

And then there is Riccardo's, more informally Ric's, and more formally Riccardo Restaurant and Gallery, and at one time it would have been a close race between Ric's and the Billy Goat for the place that serves me, a lot of newspapermen, the most drinks.

Ric's opens shortly after Prohibition's end by a man whose real name is Richard Novaretti but who has taken the more dashing name of Ric Riccardo. He has been a ship's mate, a dancer, a musician, and a painter. He comes to Chicago and, after first running a restaurant/speakeasy on south Oakley Avenue, buys the first of three buildings that will become his restaurant/bar on the corner of Rush and Hubbard Streets.

In the southernmost space, he creates a bar in the shape of an artist's palette and places above it on the wall seven murals representing the "Lively Arts": Ivan Albright's *Drama*, Aaron Bohrad's *Architecture*, Rudolph Weisenborn's

Literature, Vincent D'Agostino's *Painting,* William Schwartz's *Music,* Malvin "Zsissly" Albright's *Sculpture,* and his own *Dance.*

Ric's becomes known as the "Montmartre of the Midwest," and the nights there are a wild and wonderful, colorful and raucous mix of artists, writers, journalists, opera singers and movie stars, admen, drunks, scalawags, and bon vivants, real and would-be. It is a time when and a place where being carefree is not a sin.

My parents meet there in 1949, and I am born and walking by the time Riccardo dies in 1954, and his place is taken over by his son, Ric Jr. But he doesn't pay enough attention to it, distracted by ambitions of a career in the theater and numerous love affairs. The weight of three alimony payments and child support eventually force him to sell some of the "Lively Arts" and eventually to sell the whole joint.

Brothers Nick and Bill Angelos buy Ric's in 1974, purchasing its reputation and, in many ways, the burden of its colorful past. The "Lively Arts" are replaced by photographic reproductions, and regulars feel a terrible irony when they hear of Ric Jr.'s death in 1977: He chokes on a piece of food at a diner in a place called Buckeye, Arizona. But during the late 1970s and most of the '80s, Ric's remains a popular hangout. It is a virtual clubhouse for reporters and editors during the *Daily News*' final month in 1978. It remains a moody character as flashy, themed restaurants begin to take hold.

Sam and longtime grill man Bill Charuchas slicing onions.

It surprises few regulars in 1989 when the sale of the building is announced. That deal falls through. Another transformation—a group leases the place in 1992 and creates a short-lived, upscale dining spot with private club upstairs—drives many of the old regulars away for good and replaces the photographic "Lively Arts" murals with a large, strangely dark mural featuring a nude man, and others who resemble Nelson Algren, Mike Royko, and Studs Terkel. The Angelos brothers come back in 1993, but there is no salvation.

It ends on August 25, 1995, with a party that attracts the ruddy faces of reporters and editors. The faces of advertising

Goats occasionally visited the tavern on Hubbard Street.

and public relations men and women. The faces of some of the once young and angry reporters who founded the *Chicago Journalism Review* here in the wake of the 1968 Democratic convention. The faces of elderly blacks who continue to frequent Ric's because it was once the only downtown restaurant to serve blacks without hassle. These last-nighters have come to pay respects, perhaps to get a youthful buzz, to recall an affair, to recapture something they don't realize they are missing. You cannot move in the place.

"I hate to close," says Nick. "The taxes, they started to kill me. The taxes and the other restaurants and the fact that people don't drink like they used to. I have no choice. But, if I had crowds like this every night. . ."

I leave the party for a while and walk over to the Goat. It is empty but for a couple of tables of college kids. I find Sam. He is in a reflective mood.

"How's it going over there?" he asks and, not waiting for an answer, says, "It makes me feel older, Ric's closing. When I first come here, Ric's, it was the most famous Italian restaurant in Chicago. Friday, Saturday nights, the limousines pull up one after one. It was the top place. I eat there many times. I'm sorry it has to go."

All the other great places are gone: the Radio Grill, Corona, Boul-Mich, St. Louis Browns. But Riccardo's is reborn as Stefani's 437 in 2000, though many of us still call it Ric's. Newspaper editors and reporters still drink there; a few of us, and owner Phil Stefani appreciate the history of the place. Photos of famous Chicago journalists and writers are on the walls of the bar area, my father's among them. He has been dead for nearly 20 years, but two years ago I take my three-month-old daughter Fiona there to show her his photo. When she is 15 months old and ready for her first restaurant meal, she eats a hamburger and the top half of a bun at the Billy Goat. Sam gives her a T-shirt and a kiss on the cheek.

A Chicago Tavern

In 1967, three years after opening on Hubbard Street, Billy expands into an adjoining space to the west that had been a parking ramp. He hires workmen to put up wood paneling on the walls, and for one day at least, as *Sun-Times* columnist Tom Fitzpatrick describes it, the place "looked like your classic suburban recreation room."

In this new room, with a champagne and caviar party, Billy unveils the Wall of Fame, dominated at its center by a hand-drawn portrait of Billy that dwarfs the photos on either side. These are the faces of 37 men and one woman who were once top-ranking newspaper editors, reporters, and columnists; a couple of television personalities and one newspaper publisher; one mayor and a man who was the chauffeur for a *Tribune* editor.

There is probably not a person alive who can identify all of these faces. One might have better luck with the names above the bar on the eastern wall. Under a sign that labels them "Among the Finest" are the same number of names as people's pictures on the opposite wall, 38. All of these are the names of writers, in blown-up bylines. Most of them are dead, their names a curiosity to the tourists and most of the younger customers, even those in the media. They should know a few: still writing John Kass, Roger Ebert, Richard Roeper, Terry Armour, and Rick Telander. They might have a

47

dusty memory of some others: Jack Griffin, Condon, Kup, William Granger, Tim Weigel. But only an accomplished newspaper historian will recognize George Murray, Will Leonard, or Bernard "Beck" Beckwith.

There is only one father-son team on the wall: Herb Lyon (byline and photo) and his son Jeff (byline). Herb is dead and his son Jeff sits next to me in the Tribune Tower where he works as an editor on the staff of the magazine. In 1987 he won a Pulitzer Prize, but long before that he worked the late shift at the *Chicago American*.

"By the time I would get over to the Goat after work it was around 1 A.M., things had mostly quieted down, and it was the old man and me talking on a surprisingly straight level," he remembers. "Billy did have his reflective side, hard as that may be to believe. But on other nights, people would still be there, and we'd push tables together. The crowd consisted of Royko, of course, but also Bill Bender, the photographer, Marty O'Connor from Channel 5 . . . so many others. And, on some occasions, Condon. You could always tell when he arrived because there was something that I'd compare to a storm surge when he came in the door. You could also smell his cigar before he was fully inside. The conversations got pretty raucous and obscene."

He remembers, too, that "Billy always sat in the back with his bad leg up on a chair. He invariably wore a white shirt and dark pants. His beard was always perfectly trimmed. He mostly talked about the old days on Madison Street and the colorful guys he knew whose names meant little to me: old-time pols, fixers, cop brass, sportswriters of the past. I hope this doesn't sound too sappy, but Billy was incredibly loyal and empathetic with the people he called his friends. His showman side was really a cover. Marty O'Connor had about 10 kids, and I think Billy was helping him out a little. The thing about Billy is that he lived in this little hotel room and never spent a dime that I could tell. He didn't drink and he only wore a suit when he went to a funeral.

"Sam? I'll say this for Sam. After Billy died, I didn't think, a lot of us didn't think he'd be able to keep the place going. But he developed this keen business sense that no one knew he had. Must be in the blood."

Jeff doesn't visit the tavern often, but he was there a couple of times last year. "Any changes? Well, there was a little more grease on my dad's picture," he says.

I am sitting in the Billy Goat with Tim Weigel, a former *Daily News* sports columnist who has been successfully seduced by the money available in being a sportscaster on television. He is partial to colorful clothing, and that compels Mike to call Tim "the only Yale graduate I know who dresses like a Blue Island pimp." We notice a new name on the wall, that of a television producer we think is an idiot. She has begged Sam to put her name up.

"Your names, I want to put them on the wall," Sam says. "You go up there with Mike and all your other friends."

"Maybe later," says Tim. He doesn't want to hurt Sam's feelings by sharing our contempt for the producer. "We're just not ready yet."

Eventually the producer's name vanishes from the wall. We are not the only ones who don't like her, and Tim and I are able to meet and drink without her shadow.

He likes to talk about music and books and friends and softball. For a couple of decades, the Billy Goat sponsors softball teams, and some of their trophies still sit along the tavern's windowsill. Every few months, on a weekend morning, you will find Sam wiping dust from the trophies and saying, "One year I sponsor six different teams. Now they don't have any. Nobody likes to play, I guess. But before, all the players, they come here after the games and drink a lot of beers."

The most famous of those teams is Royko's Raiders, a group of newspapermen and a few ringers. Mike is the team's pitcher, spiritual leader, and party planner.

Tim is on those teams and so is Don DeBat, who still plays 16-inch softball a few times a week during the season and who remembers, "In early spring, the sponsorship ritual began. I usually was sent by Mike to Sam's office to pick up the softball sponsor's check. Sam's office looked like an urban renewal site. Papers stacked to the ceiling amid Goat T-shirts, and framed and ready to hang memorabilia searching for a vacant spot on the already covered walls.

"One night after a loss, we headed to the tavern to lick our wounds and gargle a few beers. After a while Sam brought a goat in for a drink. The goat smelled pretty bad and Mike kept feeding the goat $1 bills. Then some one hands Mike a $10 bill and the goat eats it. Just a couple of minutes later, the goat lets loose with a fusilade of pellets on Mike's shoes. Seeing this, Sam yells from behind the bar, 'Hey Mike. He gave you change.'

"We won the Grant Park championship — 18–1 in 1975 — and the victory party at the Goat was so wild that someone poured a pitcher of beer on Mike's head. Those were great times. Mike introduced the team to the 'Polish Depth Charge,' a shot of Christian Brothers brandy dropped, glass and all into, a stein of Billy Goat draft beer. And, of course, [reporter] Herb Gould invented the team song, *F— the F— —*."

One night in 2000 Sam and I go to the hospital to visit Tim. He is undergoing treatment for brain cancer. Sam takes one look at Tim's hospital-made chicken dinner and says, "Don't eat that. I will be right back," and he is. In less than 30 minutes he returns with waiters and a feast from one of the restaurants in nearby Greektown. The hospital room, a suite actually, is filled with family and friends and good Greek food. Looking at this scene, Tim says, "I feel like the George Bailey character played by Jimmy Stewart in *It's a Wonderful Life*. Every one of my relationships has been intensified. I know it sounds corny, but I really feel blessed."

In a cab heading back to the Goat, Sam says, "I put Tim's name on the wall now. Maybe it will help him." It doesn't. Tim dies at 56 the next year, but it is good to have his name on the wall because every time I'm in the Goat I look at his name and remember and feel better, and when Sam sees me staring at the name he puts his hand on my shoulder and says, "He was a good man, Tim, and sometimes I can hear him laughing. Your name it should be up there with Tim, with Mike."

"Maybe later," I always tell him.

"Don't wait till you die," he always says.

The question is becoming frequent: "How do you feel, Billy?"

The answer is always the same: "No good. My leg, she hurts all the time."

That leg, injured long ago when he is a newsboy and is hit by a newspaper delivery truck, is never right. There are 16 operations on it over the years, none very successful. That's why he uses a cane for decades. But he rarely complains, dismissing that ailment and the others that come at him with age. Most days he summons a favored few pals to his table in the V.I.P. (Very Insecure People) Room. And, as old men do, he tells stories of the past, of his boyhood in Greece, and the wild times on Madison Street.

These are stories those at the table know well. Most of them have told the stories in print: how one of Billy's goats escapes into the city sewer system; how, when Billy is arrested for speeding, he so charms the cop that he isn't given a ticket but rather a free lunch; how he is served with a draft notice when he was 70; about his formally applying to NASA for the first liquor license on the moon; the time he gets his shoes stolen while vacationing in Ireland; when he bails two midgets out of jail after the couple is charged with drunken driving after leaving the tavern.

They sit and laugh. They are old but they have brought the memories of that "perpetual Halloween" on Madison Street to this place and the memories sustain them.

Billy Goat dies alone in his hotel room on October 22, 1970. It is a heart attack, the doctors at Henrotin Hospital say. The papers fill with obituaries and eulogies. Condon calls Billy "the greatest American I have ever known." Others use words like "colorful," "eccentric," and "kindly old curmudgeon."

The wake, held in the chapel of Conboy Funeral Home on North Avenue, attracts hundreds of people, as does the funeral mass at St. Basil's Greek Orthodox Church on Ashland Avenue. Billy is to be buried in Greece, but the hearse carrying his body makes a detour before going to O'Hare. It first heads west and cruises by the empty lot that was the site of the old man's first tavern and then turns east toward Hubbard Street.

A few regulars, fresh from the funeral mass, stand on the sidewalk outside and raise their glasses as the hearse passes. The Billy Goat is closed. There is a big wreath on the front door. The drinks have come from Riccardo's, just up the street.

One man is not drinking. Sachio Yamashita, who everyone calls Sachi, is painting rainbow colors on the dreary exterior walls of the Goat. He tells Billy, "The top of Michigan Avenue is the most beautiful street in the world. But every day I walk down here with all this filth and all the pigeons and it is most depressing." Billy makes a deal: every day after Sachi and his helpers finish their work, beer and hamburgers are free.

So, there is Sachi working, telling columnist Tom Fitzpatrick, "I did not make it to the funeral. I want to get this job finished. Wherever Billy Goat is, I think he understands that."

The hearse passes, and a *Tribune* reporter, an old friend of my father's, hands me something, and says, "Here. The old goat wrote this to the *Tribune* a few months ago. Read it. It's not a bad epitaph."

The letter reads: "When I arrived in Chicago from Greece in 1912, I applied for citizenship. I knew a good country when I saw it and I became a modest, loyal and accurate American."

Mike is the first person Sam calls after finding Billy's body, and his column in that day's paper begins, "Billy Goat's Tavern closed at 2 this morning, but as usual the old man with the white beard, the bad leg, and the cane didn't want to go home.

"It wasn't until after three that William (Billy Goat) Sianis, the city's greatest tavern keeper, would stop talking and allow his nephew, Sam, to help him into his car and drive a few blocks to the St. Clair Hotel, where he lived. Then he went to his room, fell over, and died. It was typical of Billy Goat that he would die during the only five hours of the day when his place wasn't open for business. That's how good a businessman he was."

Mike writes that the only criticism he had of Billy was that he kept a goat instead of what Mike considered the more traditional tavern creature, "a black-tongued dog trained to bite the throats of burglars and nip the behinds of brawlers."

He has discussed this matter with Billy, who said, "I'll tell you why I don't have a dog. I had a dog once. But he bit a customer and I had to pay all the medical bills. The customer was the kind of bum who drank nothing but martinis, and so naturally the dog got sick, and I had to pay his medical bills, too. That's why I prefer goats. Besides, if things get real tough, you can get milk from a goat. You can even make a good stew from a goat. What can you do with an old dog?"

Mike ends the column with this: "The whole city should take a few minutes off and go in a tavern and have a drink to the memory of Billy Goat, a fine old dog."

Three years after his uncle's death, Sam comes to Wrigley Field for a July 4, 1973, game between the Cubs and Philadelphia Phillies. He arrives in a black limousine driven by Fabulous Howard, the flamboyant owner of a limo service. Condon who, not coincidentally, is along for the ride, describes the car as looking like "the Chicago Stadium with chrome." When it pulls into a spot reserved for that devoted White Sox fan, Mayor Richard J. Daley, it is quickly surrounded by police officers, security personnel, and Andy Frain ushers.

Fabulous Howard unfurls a red carpet for Sam and the goat, but before they reach its end, they are told, "Tickets or not, no goat is getting into Wrigley."

Sam walks from gate to gate with the goat, named Socrates, who is wearing a hand-painted sign that reads, "All is Forgiven. Let Me Lead You to the Pennant. Your friend, Billy Goat."

"When they refuse us, I try more gates and nothing happened," says Sam. "Except then the pitcher, Ferguson Jenkins, I guess he hears about us, and he comes out there and he is very happy that we can break the curse, and he offers to take me and the goat into the clubhouse. But then the security, they close the door for us and even for the great Ferguson Jenkins. But he shakes my hand and he shakes Socrates' foot."

A few days later, a new photo goes up on the walls of the bar. "I put up the great pitcher, Ferguson Jenkins," Sam says. "He was the only one to understand. So, whenever he pitches, the curse will not be in effect."

The next year Sam tries to buy Cubs season tickets for himself and a goat. "They want to give a season ticket for me but refuse the goat," he tells *Daily News* sportswriter David Israel. "So I told them they don't accept me either. You saw what happened this year." The 1974 season ended with the Cubs at 66–96, 22 games out.

The American League champion that year is the Oakland A's, owned by fun-loving iconoclast Charlie Finley, a frequent visitor to the Billy Goat and an animal lover who often parades his mule, Charley O., at Oakland games. He and Sam first meet in 1970, and for the next four years Socrates lives with Charley O. on Finley's farm in La Porte, Indiana. It is Finley's idea to ship Charley O. and Socrates, as well as Sam, out to Oakland to await the A's return from the first two Series games in Los Angeles against the Dodgers. At the game, Sam and the goat parade around the field. The A's win the series, and back in Chicago, Sam says, "I hope the Cubs learn and they let me in opening day in '75. So we can see a World Series here. I don't like flying so much."

Mike is concerned as he watches "many young ladies, and some who weren't too young, coming to the tavern and making goo-goo eyes" at Sam in the wake of Billy's death and with the news that Sam has inherited the bar.

Mike writes: "I urged him to go back to his native Greece and find a nice girl who knows nothing of checking accounts, charge accounts, Bonwit Teller, Gloria Steinem, tennis clubs, and property laws. My motives were partly selfish. Billy Goat is my favorite tavern, and a tavern is only as happy as its owner, and a tavern owner cannot be happy with a wife who expects him home before 3 A.M."

That "native girl" is Irene Dariotis. Mike meets her on the phone. Sam is in Greece and he says to Mike, "Irene is right here with me. We gonna get married next week. Here, I put her on the phone. Irene, say hallo."

"Hallo," she says.

"Hello," Mike says. "Are you looking forward to the wedding?"

"Hallo," says Irene.

"Do you think you will like Chicago?" says Mike.

"Hallo," says Irene.

Sam gets back on the phone and says, "Her English ain't too good yet."

Sam and Irene are married in Greece in November 1974. Above the cash register in the Billy Goat is a lovely and large photo of Sam dancing at his wedding, a very happy tavern owner.

Bill Murray is hungry and that is why we are walking toward one of the Goat's red-and-white-checkered tables. He is here in June 1999 to promote a book he has written, *Cinderella Story: My Life in Golf.* Waiter Tito Chacon recognizes him immediately.

"Bill Murray," he says. "You are the funniest."

"The funniest what?" says Murray.

Sam sees Murray and walks over. The two men hug.

"How's your oldest boy?" asks Sam.

"He's huge," says Murray, whose two grown sons have been coming to the Goat since they were kids. "He could swallow both of us. All he needs is a couple of tattoos."

The two men talk for a while. A couple of pictures are taken.

"I saw that new place of yours over by the United Center," Murray says. "For a minute I thought they'd run you out of here."

"No, no," says Sam. "I always will have this place."

"Sam, you're the most successful Greek in the world," Murray says.

"You help make that happen," says Sam.

"Don't blame me," says Murray.

A
CURSE

Sam and sons Tom and Bill try again to break the curse.

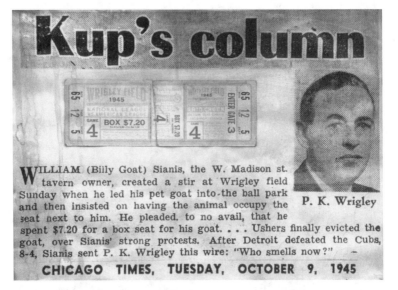

Kup's column

WILLIAM (Billy Goat) Sianis, the W. Madison st. tavern owner, created a stir at Wrigley field Sunday when he led his pet goat into-the ball park and then insisted on having the animal occupy the seat next to him. He pleaded. to no avail, that he spent $7.20 for a box seat for his goat. . . . Ushers finally evicted the goat, over Sianis' strong protests. After Detroit defeated the Cubs, 8-4, Sianis sent P. K. Wrigley this wire: "Who smells now?"

P. K. Wrigley

CHICAGO TIMES, TUESDAY, OCTOBER 9, 1945

Columnist Irv Kupcinet was one of two reporters to mention what would be one of the most infamous events in Chicago sports history.

WE GOT DETROIT'S GOAT

Billy and a gang of Andy Frain ushers recreate the day Billy and his goat were barred from game 4 of the Cubs-Detroit series.

CHICAGO DAILY
SUN ⏲ TIMES
THE PICTURE NEWSPAPER
FRIDAY, SEPTEMBER 22, 1950

Chicago Briefs
'Hex' Gets Wrigley's Goat—Now All's Well

After thinking it over for five years, President Philip K. Wrigley of the Chicago Cubs decided he was the goat when he refused to admit a goat to the 1945 World Series.

The goat is Murphy, one of the pets of William (Billy Goat) Sianis, owner of Billy Goat Inn at 1855 W. Madison.

Philip K. Wrigley

Gene Kessler, SUN - TIMES sports columnist, recently printed a letter in which Sianis said Murphy was ready to accept an apology and take the hex off the Cubs.

Thursday Sianis read Murphy a letter from Wrigley, saying:

"Will you please extend to him (Murphy) my most sincere and abject apologies . . . and ask him not only to remove the 'hex' but to reverse the flow and start pulling for wins?"

The letter was written Sept. 12. Since then the Cubs have won several games.

William (Billy Goat) Sianis shows his goat the letter of apology from Philip K. Wrigley.

Until this 1950 story, there had been no mention of a curse, a hex, or a jinx beyond the chatty confines of the tavern.

Goats eventually made it onto the field, but to no avail.

Two years after Billy's death, Sam and a goat, along with sportswriter Dave Condon (right, with ever-present cigar) and limo driver "Fabulous" Howard, head to a game at Wrigley Field.

Sam is interviewed by Cubs broadcaster Harry Caray.

Sam's oldest sons, Bill and Tom, spent much of their youth in taverns and playing with goats.

Cubs great Ernie Banks, retired for more then 20 years, leads Sam and a goat along the warning track before a game in 1994.

George Motz is sitting in the Billy Goat saying that the origin of ground beef can be traced to nomadic Mongolian and Tartar warriors who tenderized meat by putting it under the saddles of their horses while riding into battle.

The origin of the hamburger, he says, is a bit harder to pin down. He mentions some of the places that can lay claim to inventing the hamburger and says there is no doubt who invented the cheeseburger: a man named Louis Ballast who owned a Humpty Dumpty Barrel Drive-In in Denver. The simplicity of it all: One day he puts a slice of cheese on the burger as it cooks, likes the taste, and immediately applies for a patent. That is in March 1935, the year Sam is born.

"So, probably that guy who invents the cheeseburger . . . maybe in his mind he says, 'One of these days a guy he might come here to the Unites States from Greece and make the cheeseburger famous," Sam says.

Motz spends two years making a documentary titled *Hamburger America*. He calls it "a celebration of burgers and the people who make them." This is his criteria: Each place has to have fresh meat, nothing frozen; has to be family-owned for more than 40 years; has to have had the same burger on the menu for all those years; the burgers have to be distinctive; and the restaurants have to have a good story. After a year of traveling and eating, he selects seven places.

"All roads led to the Goat," says Motz, born and raised and still living in the New York City area. "I had never heard of the place, but most people in the burger world kept saying, 'The Goat has got to be in there.' The first time I came for a visit, I had a hard time even finding it. I was lost for a while, just wandering the bowels of Chicago. But that first cheeseburger . . . "

It is lunchtime. Jammed and noisy. Spiro Sarivasilis, who works the grill from early morning to mid-afternoon, is shouting, "Cheezborger, cheezborger . . . Doublecheez the best . . . Don't look at the menu. I am the menu today."

Bartender Jeff Magill is asked, "What it is about burgers?"

"They are round and they fit in your hands," he says. "They are ergonomically correct. But there's something else. It's just a theory, but I think that the first meal that most kids have outside the home is a burger, and that makes them a modern archetype."

Sam, about to go help on the grill, says, "So, what it is about burgers? People like them. They like them because they're good."

January 28, 1978, and *Saturday Night Live* is on TV, and there is Bill Murray playing a waiter named Nico Dionasopolis. He is standing behind a diner's counter nodding agreeably as guest host Robert Klein says,

"I'll have a couple of eggs and sausage — is that link sausage or patty? [Nico nods] Link? [Nico nods] Link? [Nico nods] Uh, link sausage, a large orange juice, and coffee."

Murray: "Cheeseburger?"

Klein: "No, I don't want a cheeseburger. Eggs, couple of eggs. [Nico nods] Eggs. [Nico nods] Do you speak English? [Nico nods] Eggs, couple of eggs, over lightly, with sausage."

John Belushi, as diner owner Pete Dionasopolis, interrupts: "No, no, no, no, no eggs — cheeseburger!"

Klein: "When do you stop serving breakfast?"

Belushi: "Now. No breakfast."

Klein: "No breakfast?"

Belushi: "Nope."

Klein: "I just want a couple of eggs."

Belushi: "No breakfast! Cheeseburger!"

Klein: "Shut up! I don't want a cheeseburger!"

Belushi: "Come on, come on, come on — don't give me that. Come on, let's go, let's go, we gotta have turnover! You want a cheeseburger? Everybody got a cheeseburger, you want a cheeseburger? Come on — cheeseburger?"

Klein: "I don't want a cheeseburger! I just got up, it's too early for a cheeseburger!"

Belushi: "Too early for cheeseburger? Look! [He points around to his customers] Cheeseburger, cheeseburger, cheeseburger, cheeseburger, cheeseburger, cheeseburger,

cheeseburger, cheeseburger, cheeseburger, cheeseburger, cheeseburger, cheeseburger, cheeseburger."

The skit continues. "Cheeseburger" is spoken 80 times.

Sam doesn't see this. He learns about the first Olympia Diner skit a few days after it airs, when he attends the retirement party of a *Tribune* reporter. "The people at the party, they are screaming, 'Cheezborger, cheezborger.' I didn't know why. But they say, 'They have you on TV,' and explain about the *Saturday Night* show. Any place I start to go, people see me and say, 'Say it . . . say it. Say 'Cheezborger . . . Cheezborger.' We become pretty famous pretty fast."

There was no food served in the original tavern on Madison Street, but on the day the Goat opens on Hubbard Street its most popular menu item is one that is referred to as a "double-hamburger-on-toasted-roll-with-chopped-onions-and-relish."

But with Sam working the grill, the place begins to echo with his distinctive pitch to customers walking down the stairs: "Cheezborger, Cheezborger! No fries, chips! No Pepsi, Coke!"

The lunch crowd is then much as it is now, but with fewer tourists: a mix of construction workers, men and women from nearby office buildings, the press. In the late 1960s, it becomes a favorite lunch stop for a shaggy-haired advertising copywriter named Don Novello. He works for Leo Burnett in the Prudential Building, a few blocks south across the river. Billy doesn't like Novello and sometimes smacks him with his cane or his toy hammer and shouts, "Get a haircut."

After leaving Chicago, Novello becomes a *Saturday Night Live* staff writer. Two weeks into the job he transforms his Billy Goat experiences into a skit that calls for the most elaborate set the show had ever had, because it includes a working grill. Some of the cast members and producers aren't enthusiastic about the skit but John Belushi— "Because he knew the Billy Goat too," says Novello—was, and only asks that the place be called the Olympia Diner in honor of his father Adam, who has run such a place.

In a remarkable but typically Chicago confluence, Mike Royko knows Belushi from the time he is a little boy, and when the comic dies in 1982, Mike writes about those days decades before, "sitting in a short-order diner in Logan Square . . . [and] John's Uncle Pete would be at the grill, slapping cheeseburgers on the grill, jiggling the fries . . . I don't remember if Pete said 'chizbooga' and 'cheeps' exactly the way John did later. His accent was Albanian, not Greek. But it was close.

"And somewhere in another neighborhood, in another short-order joint, Adam Belushi was slapping cheeseburgers on another grill. Everybody in the family was chasing the American dream."

He writes about the evenings he spent with the Belushi brothers "drinking Metaxa and talking about the things we might do some day"; about the Belushis later opening their "dream restaurant [with] thick carpets and cloth wallpaper, oil paintings, a piano player in the bar, and the best prime rib I've ever had"; and about the last time he sees John. Then he ends the column, "[John] was only thirty-three. I learned a long time ago that life isn't always fair. But it shouldn't cheat that much."

Twenty-five years behind a bar will teach you a great deal about mankind. Not all of it will be good, but much of it will be interesting, and some of it will be important.

Jeff Magill comes to the Billy Goat with what might be the perfect background for tending bar. He is a clinical specialist for the inpatient psychiatric department of Illinois Masonic and Barclay hospitals.

He has spent some time moonlighting as a bartender as a way to put some extra money into his pocket as he and his wife Lydia begin to start a family. "And for a while I spent considerable time on the other side of the bar, too," he says. But he has never been in the Billy Goat until the March day in 1981 when he walks in to apply for a job. "I had seen it whenever I took a shortcut along lower Wacker Drive and turned onto lower Michigan. It started to become for me a kind of secret reward of crossing the bridge. It was always this kind of mysterious place."

That March day he parks nearby, walks in, and tells Sam he wants a job.

Sam says, "Where you work before?"

"I work at Armando's and at the Sign of the Trader. That's where a lot of the commodities traders go. I can work as fast as anybody," Jeff tells Sam.

Sam takes his name and number down on a piece of paper, and two days later calls and says, "You the guy who work in the hospital? I want you to start Tuesday. Maybe you should wear a tie. I think it will make you better tips."

So there he is, serving his first customer, who is still a customer, one of the bar's most durable regulars. Let's call him Bill.

"I knew the kid would make it," says Bill. "He poured a good beer."

Two days on the new job and Jeff gets rid of his tie.

"But that first Friday the place is a madhouse, and later Sam tells me, 'We break the record today. Highest lunch sales ever,'" Jeff says. "That's when I thought I might be part of something big here."

Before the start of the 1984 season, the Cubs' general manager, Dallas Green, walks into the tavern. "I was here that day and he came down and talked to Sam directly, kind of pleading," says Jeff. "It was 'All is forgiven. Please bring the goat.'"

Sam does, on opening day, and announcer Jack Brickhouse presides at a ceremony on the pitching mound where Sam and the goat renounce the curse.

The Cubs do well, winning the National League East and beating the NL West's San Diego Padres 13–0 and 4–2 in Chicago before losing three in a row on the road.

"Maybe they should have invited the goat to San Diego," says Jeff.

There is much debate at the tavern in 1984 about the curse. Those who do not believe say, "It's stupid, a bunch of silly nonsense to explain the Cubs inadequacies," or "Curses are for Oil Can Harry—all cartoony nonsense. But it's nice to give serial ineptitude an identity more colorful than 'serial ineptitude.'"

Arguing persuasively for the curse is *Sun-Times* sports columnist Ray Sons. He knows the Billy Goat well and remembers: "While sports editor of the *Daily News* I covered every Bear game in company with the beat reporter and two photographers. We did pages of photos, stories, and commentary for our Monday editions in a fashion that seems ludicrous now in this age of television overkill. Then middle-aged, instead of lapsing into senility as now, I still had the strength to fly home from a road game, write 600-800 words, spend an hour or more viewing photos with the photogs in the darkroom and brief night copy desk on what we should display. With an hour left before closing time at the Goat, I'd stagger gratefully alone into that subterranean den and order a double cheeseburger and a boilermaker (shot of Early Times and a mug of beer). A second boilermaker would sufficiently subdue my jangled nerves to allow me to climb aboard the 'L' and reach the Fullerton stop within walking distance of the home I inhabited for a couple of years. I was between marriages at the time, so there was no wife to berate me for floundering home so late and smelling of the Goat's produce."

In 1984 he writes of the curse: "After all, Billy Goat Sianis had died, so that wasn't the original Sianis or the original goat on the mound. Under law of the land, Sam Sianis could and did inherit a saloon from his uncle, but does the power to remove a curse pass from generation to generation, even outside the immediate family, from uncle to nephew? I think not.

"A source close to the late Sianis and who remains a confidant of his nephew assures me the goat that stood on the mound . . . wasn't even a relative of the original goat [that was] eaten by members of the Sianis clan or their friends and never had the opportunity to remove its part of the hex, or authorize a latter-day goat to dismiss it . . . No, I maintain Billy Goat's curse lives."

Mike writes about the Goat often, sometimes using it as the setting for conversations with his fictional alter ego, the barstool philosopher, Slats Grobnik. He also writes columns about Sam, about the day he meets and serves Super Drunk, a man who is in the tavern for 12 hours one Saturday and consumes 150 shots of whiskey mixed with ginger ale ("I swear it is true," Sam tells Mike), or about the time Sam "bounced the same drunken brawler out of his tavern six times in the same night."

Mike also captures a short conversation in 1987, when he warns Sam that "times were changing and he should consider changing with them."

"Ferns, Sam, you had better think about ferns."

"How you cook dem?" Sam asks.

"You don't cook them. They're plants. You hang them from the walls and ceilings."

Sam shakes his head and says, "No plants een dees place. Plants got bugs. I no like bugs."

One of Mike's most famous columns is about the 1991 day Sam meets a president.

"It was a big day," says Sam. "I come in early that morning and I see two guys in suits just looking around the place.

I ask if they need help and they say no so I just do what I always do and then go to a lunch meeting. I'm there and I get a call and they say Bush is coming. I am shocked and I hurry back and they are all getting ready for the president. When he gets there he eats and sits with me and four regular customers and talks about family and politics. He wants to know the history of the Billy Goat and he wants to know about Mike."

Sam calls Mike and excitedly tells his assistant over the phone, "The president wants to know if Mike is here. I tell him no and then he wants to know where he usually sit and I show him and he seems very excited to see where he sit when he come down here."

Sam wants Mike to have a burger with Bush. He says no. Sam calls Mike's wife, Judy. She wants him to go. He says no. Mike often refers to Bush as "the greatest tourist of our time," and in the next day's *Tribune* writes, "The country is going to hell in a hand basket, and the president of the United States wants to know on what part of the bar I rest my elbows? Or forehead?"

One thing that Mike writes about Sam is never published. It is a recommendation letter. Sam can't remember what it is for, but in it Mike writes, "I've known Sam Sianis for many years and consider him one of my closest friends. He has so many fine qualities, many of them sadly lacking in our present society, that I'm not sure where to start, but I'll try.

Long after writing the *Saturday Night Live* skits that made the Billy Goat famous, Don Novello returns to visit with Sam and Bill.

"Work ethic: If everyone in this country tended to their jobs or businesses with Sam's diligence, Japan would be up to its collective ears in red ink. Since taking over Billy Goat's Tavern, he has turned it into one of the country's best-known bars. He treats his employees fairly and earns their loyalty. In a time when many in the service industry don't seem to know the meaning of service, Sam and his staff treat all of his customers alike, whether they are famous or an old bag lady who wants to sit in the corner to get out of the cold. With courtesy, congeniality, promptness, and a fair deal. [That bag lady, incidentally, never went away hungry or without a warming cup of coffee].

Some of the lively regulars spreading out from Wise Guy's
Corner.

"He's a man of good humor. I've never once heard him
grump or grouch about the steep price of success. Just the
opposite. He glories in hard work and challenge.

"It would be redundant to say that's he's an astute businessman. His bottom line will tell you that.

"Most important, though, Sam is an honorable man. If
he says he will do something, you can count on it. If we all
treated others as honestly as Sam does, half the law schools
would be closed.

"In closing, I would say that if I had to walk down to the
OK Corral, Sam would be the first person I'd ask to join me.

On second thought, I wouldn't have to ask. He'd already be there."

"It's after closing and nobody's in here, and I see Mike when he is dead," Sam says. "He had some kind of pile of papers in front of him and he's looking at the papers. I see that he is crying, and I say, 'What happens, Mike? Is anything wrong?' And he says, 'No, no, Sam, I just miss my wife.' And then he get up, walk up the stairs out the door."

Mike spends a lot of time at the Billy Goat, and a lot of other bars, after the sudden death of his first wife, Carol, in 1978. He is angry, guilty, sad, and, when it is late and there have been too many drinks, he talks seriously of suicide.

He pulls out of it, gets back to work, dates a lot of women, tries to be a good father to his two grown sons. In 1982 he meets Judy Arndt, a pretty, smart, and understanding blond. She teaches him to play tennis. He takes her to the Billy Goat.

"A night was just not complete for him without a stop at the Goat," says Judy. "I think a lot of it had to do with the fact that the Goat, with its tired linoleum floor, its lack of anything fancy, its lack of pretension, took him back to his childhood before he was famous and everybody wanted a piece of him. And after Carol died, I think he came there so often because he just didn't want to be alone. And he knew Sam would not let anything bad happen to him in the Goat."

Mike and Judy are sitting in the tavern on the night the Cubs clinch the 1984 division title. The place is very crowded, and as people gravitate toward Mike to exchange high-fives, he gently takes Judy by the hand and leads her away from the bar and up the stairs. "I thought we were going to go home, but, instead, when we got outside, he takes me in his arms and we start to dance, there alone in the middle of Hubbard Street, just twirling in that strange, otherworldly light," she says. "So happy."

There are a few newspaper people who still drop in to the Goat frequently enough that Tito, Marko, Payne, Tarik, Al, Bouch, Robert, or one of the other waiters deliver our cocktails of choice without the messy chore of having to order. And sometimes, when too many of those cocktails come and go, we can fall into a kind of sappy nostalgia, recalling nights long ago when we are younger and less burdened by life.

"Do you remember . . . ?" someone will say.

"I remember that night . . . " someone will say, and what follows is some lively, evocative tale of the night Mike decides to retire to Ireland (he doesn't), or the night he and Oakland A's owner Charlie Finley hatch a plan to buy the Cubs (they don't), or of Dick McCormick of the United Press flicking his cigarette ashes on the floor, or the *Sun-Times'* Dick Mitchell and Sharon Barrett falling in love, though not with each other.

"I remember . . . I miss . . .," someone will say, and names and faces begin to float through the tavern air. Always good for a smile is Bill Charuchas, dead five years now, but so alive during the 37 years he works at the Billy Goat flipping burgers (he coined the now familiar phrase "Try the double cheese. It's the best"), giving free bags of chips to kids, flirting with girls, and drinking beer (the *Tribune's* John Kass, who has written often about the Billy Goat, estimates that Bill drank 7.4 beers a day during his years at the Billy Goat, a stunning 100,000 total).

There are other faces and voices, too, for a good tavern is the sum of collective conversations and characters, former friends, long gone, in loud confrontations or lengthy embraces, and bodies in a few real fights. Yes, that happens, but the Billy Goat functions more effectively as relatively peaceful neutral ground. As editors and executives fight quiet wars from their offices, the Billy Goat is where the troops come to unwind, bitch, moan, forget.

Reporters and booze, it's a failing marriage. The role of alcohol in the ongoing opera that is Chicago journalism is now little more than a bit player. You can still find a writer or editor or photographer sitting at the bar. You might find a bunch of us pushing tables together. But there's usually a good reason, a celebration or a goodbye, rather than because it is Tuesday, Wednesday, Thursday. Now, days can go by without any of us showing up.

It starts, or seems to, when *Chicago Today* folds in 1974, the *Daily News* four years later. And, of course, as the newspaper crowds start getting smaller, so does the fame of the place start attracting new customers, so many that by 1991, Mike writes: "Tourists. [The Billy Goat] used to be a really good bar before it became famous and tourists started coming in. You could always find an empty stool and probably sit next to an inky pressman from one of the papers, a bleary reporter, a night watchman, a cop, or a bag lady. Then John Belushi did his 'cheezbooger' routine on *Saturday Night Live*. So the yuppies started coming in to hear authentic Greek burger flippers yell cheezbooger. Then came the celebrities and tourists."

There is another reason, too. On the night that Riccardo's closes in 1995, one of its owners, Nick Angelos, says "people don't drink like they used to."

A reporter puts it bluntly, "Nobody gets drunk any more."

"This place was largely supported by its regulars," says bartender Jeff. "But by the late '80s, the number of newspaper people who would come in every single day started to diminish, and some of the others just died off or got sober. There are still a few who I'd call regulars, or let's say semi-regulars, but it's really the tourists and the casual visitors who keep the place thriving."

But when a few of us show up and get together, the past is present. There is no real melancholy shadowing our memories, but there is always the tendency to romanticize the past, and I suppose we do.

But we are not the first. Long before, Jack Griffin gets romantic about his Billy Goat past in the *Sun-Times* one day in 1969: "How the years do drift away from a man. It was such a long time ago, such a very long time ago, and so many things have come and gone since then.

"There were some great newspaper names that hung around the old place. Names the kids wouldn't know now. And maybe, outside the racket itself, not many would have known them. But they were great ones.

"It seemed newspaper people laughed a lot more then, and told more funny stories, or maybe the world didn't seem that serious then. Or maybe we didn't take it so seriously.

"Maybe they should have, and then maybe there would have been fewer torches for the new crew of torch bearers to wear. But it was the way they were, and they never left the world any worse for their trip through it. And there were some tall men among them, and they left their own heritage."

The 1994 season begins badly. The Cubs lose 12 home games in a row, the worst start in team history. In an effort to end this streak, Sam takes his goat to Wrigley Field, only to be denied entrance. Amidst the chant of "Let the Goat in!" from the crowd, Hall-of-Famer Ernie Banks escorts Sam and his goat into Wrigley. The Cubs win the game 5–2 but finish 49–64 and in fifth place in the strike-shortened season. The next year, also shortened by the strike, they go 73–71, finishing third. In 1996: 76–86, fourth place.

Ironically, but fittingly, Mike's final column is about the curse; the first column he ever writes is, fittingly, about a tavern. In that last column, which runs on March 21, 1997, he writes, "It's about time that we stopped blaming the failings of the Cubs on a poor, dumb creature that is a billy goat.

"This has been going on for years, and it has reached the point where some people actually believe it . . . It's an entertaining story, but is only partly true.

"Yes, blame for many of the Cubs' failings since 1945 can be placed on a dumb creature. Not a poor, dumb creature but a rich one.

"I'm talking about P.K. Wrigley, head of the chewing gum company, and the owner of the Cubs until he died in 1977."

He goes on to suggest the reason was racism: "If not Wrigley's, then that of the stiffs he hired to run his baseball operation . . . By 1947, the year [Jackie] Robinson broke in, the

Cubs were already pathetic doormats . . . It was not until September 1953 — nearly seven full seasons after Robinson arrived — that Wrigley signed two black players.

"By the time Cubs management got over their racial fears, the black league was getting ready to fold. Fewer players were available and better teams competed for them. Other sports, college and pro, began going after black athletes.

"So what might have been wasn't. It had nothing to do with a goat's curse. Not unless the goat wore a gabardine suit and sat behind a desk in an executive suite."

If you are a Billy Goat regular you should know at least some of these things: What Jeff likes to do in the mornings before coming to work; the favorite hobby of Nick Kapranos, the night bartender; which *Tribune* reporters removed *Sun-Times* columnist Neil Steinberg's byline from the wall; where Charlotte's is; what Gene and Barbara talk about at their table; who is Big Pete and who is Little Pete; what Chris does for a living, and Coates too; who met Frank Sinatra buying socks in Las Vegas; Skates' real name; the Cowboy's favorite drink, besides beer; the names of at least one of B.J.'s kids; the size of Bob's boat; Kathleen's e-mail address. Does your heart break when you hear of Bill Reilly's death?

"There really is no pure way these days to define a regular," says Jeff. "There are people who show up only once a year, like this guy who comes in from England to see Sox games and drink here. In a sense he's a regular. And people who visit every few weeks, they'd qualify. The guy who used to be here every night, but then got married and moved to the suburbs, but now brings his kids in every few months. Is he a regular? Yes."

Two people who qualify under any definition of "regulars" are . . . well, let's call them Bill and John. Bill has been coming to the Billy Goat for almost 30 years. He is the first customer Jeff ever serves. John has been coming here for 25 years.

They are here every morning for coffee. They, John more so than Bill, are here almost every day for a late lunch. They are here almost every night at 5:05 — you can set your clock — sitting on stools in Wise Guy's corner and talking with pals and strangers.

People come to the Goat for a variety of reasons, not the least of which is to find shelter from whatever storms are raging in their personal or professional lives, or may be afflicting the city, the planet, or any of any number of sports teams. This is a place where they can reassure or comfort themselves in conversation about matters large and small, telling stories that are real even if they aren't true. It's all a means of fighting the loneliness everyone feels.

Sam chats up the lunch crowd as Bill Charuchas works the grill.

We are lucky here. Chicago has a rich and lengthy tradition of saloons catering to most of our entertainment, cultural, and emotional needs. Ever since early settler Marc Beaubien enlivens his Sauganash Inn with fine fiddle playing in the 1830s, taverns function as important social focal points, though few are willing to admit — or understand — their significance. The best of these places survive thanks to a delicate alchemy based on booze. It levels life's playing field, and so on any night at the Billy Goat, or often during the day, you will find a CEO in heated discussion with a riverboat deckhand over the relative merits of a Supreme Court nominee; a reporter discussing I R A s with a construction worker; a lim-

Mike Royko (back row, second from right), Don DeBat (back row, third from left), Tim Weigel (front row, far right) and other members of Royko's Raiders celebrate delivery of another trophy.

ousine driver talking baseball with a teenager, who, having failed to fool Jeff with a fake ID, is sullenly sipping a Coke.

Like his uncle, Sam runs a tavern where every person is equal, where no one feels slighted, allowing the Billy Goat to function as a sanitarium and sometimes even as a home.

Jeff is talking one afternoon about some of the regulars, about the roller-skating hooker taken in by a regular, but especially about Hank Oettinger, who dies at 92 in 2004, but who makes a stop at the Billy Goat every afternoon for decades before that. "He was determined, I think, to do his bit to keep the neighborhood tavern alive. This wasn't his first stop, but he felt these places needed him. It was like he was watering a garden. And he celebrated intellect and people who were not boring."

Around 1950, there were almost 7,000 taverns in Chicago. In 2006, there were fewer than 1,250. Where do the people go? Many still come here and they see photographs of Hank and so many other regulars tightly gathered on the walls in the Wise Guy's corner and anyone sitting there will be happy to tell you about them, about taverns.

"So many stories. All of that is in the walls, in the air," says Jeff. "I will tell you a story. When my first son, John, was born we had the baptism at a church in Norwood Park. The reverend and I were talking. I hadn't seen Reverend Felt in quite a while. He started talking about good taverns, and said, 'There is more good fellowship in a lot of taverns than there ever has been in church.' He was right and that has become more and more apparent over the years. The guys who gather here with regularity, I really think they would do anything for one another. There is real affection here, and that is a very sustaining thing."

In 1998, the Cubs finish the season with 89 wins, tied with the San Francisco Giants for the wild card. During the tie-breaking game on September 28, the Cubs invite Sam and a goat to the game. The Cubs win 5–3 and go into the post season as a wild card. But the Cubs are swept in Atlanta and swept out of the post-season.

"Maybe they should have invited the goat to Atlanta," says Jeff.

Before of the 2003 season, with experts predicting a Cubs pennant, Sam says, "I'm waiting for the Cubs owner or manager to call me. They have to let the goat go in for it to work, so we could help bring the pennant and World Series here to Chicago."

Sun-Times sports columnist Rick Telander stirs up some trouble during spring training by asking manager Dusty Baker about the goat and the curse. "I don't care about no goat," snaps Baker. "I like goat milk . . . I eat goat!"

Telander contacts Sam for his reaction: "He should be careful about the goat. Aw, goats. Listen, no, they don't hurt anybody, they give everything to people. They give milk for babies and skin for shoes, and they fertilize the grass. And like Billy, he looked like a goat . . . I like the Cobs. But they blow it themselves. Always they do. Mr. Baker, he should have the goat as a friend, not a meal."

Throughout the late season, Sam is besieged by local and national media outlets for interviews. "When the goat is happy, he brings the Cubs good luck. When he's disappointed, they lose," says Sam.

With the Cubs making it into post season play, Sam understandably expects a call from Cubs management, an invitation perhaps to the sixth game of the National League divisional series with the Florida Marlins. The team has every right to be confident: up three games to two, Mark Prior on the mound. But there is no call, no invitation. So Sam and his sons Bill and Tom get themselves a goat and drive to Wrigley Field.

"We all have tickets but they would not let the goat in," says Bill. "And well . . ."

And well, the game is going fine until the eighth inning: Cubs ahead 3-1 with one out, five outs away from a World Series. But then a young man named Steve Bartman makes an enthusiastic grab for a foul ball also coveted by right fielder Moises Alou. This begins a series of unfortunate events that lead to a painful 8-3 loss and well . . .

The most successful of the Billy Goat outposts is on Navy Pier. Habitués of the Hubbard Street oasis are shocked by the airy and bright space, windows facing south to water and sky. Sunlight never brightens the windows on Hubbard Street.

The other outposts have their charms, pieces of history, and photos to remind visitors of the curse and *Saturday Night Live* and the fame of the Billy Goat. They also have french fries and broiled chicken sandwiches. In short, they are not the Billy Goat on Hubbard Street.

"I do not change anything here," says Sam of Hubbard Street. "Once I change the tiles on the floor, but that's it. I do this for my uncle."

It is easy to imagine how this would please old Billy Goat, as well as how famous his nephew has become: the frequent mentions of Sam and his establishments in the newspapers and on TV; Sam featured in ads for the Illinois Lottery and commercials for Old Style. He would be happy that the place continues to attract actors and athletes and celebrities. He would be very happy to learn that Hillary Clinton, when First Lady, has a private party at the Billy Goat and that she, a native of Park Ridge, knows all the history and lore of the place; that Bill Clinton, when he is president, pays a visit to the Billy Goat's booth at Taste of Chicago; how many times the mayors Daley drop in, along with so many lesser known politicians, real and aspiring.

When the Billy Goat opens in Washington, D.C., I write an item for the *Tribune*. There is a story in the *Sun-Times*. There is an editorial in the *Tribune*: "Even if the Billy Goat is ready for Washington, is Washington ready for 'the Goat,' as generations of Chicago news folks have known it?" There is nothing in the Washington newspapers.

The National Association of Realtors building in which the new Billy Goat sits is dramatic: 12 stories sheathed in blue-green glass topped by a tower that extends 40 feet above the official District of Columbia height line. Its shape is that of an acute triangle, not unlike New York City's famous Flatiron Building, narrowing to eight feet at its north end.

A *Chicago Tavern*

The design is driven in part by the NAR's pursuit of a
green building certification through the U.S. Green Building
Council, a coalition of building industry leaders committed
to using environmentally friendly materials and features. Less
than 100 buildings have been so certified and this one is.

Sam's son, Bill, is in Washington into 2006, running the
place, living in a nearby hotel, lonely but busy. Some nights,
when the weather is gentle, Bill rides an elevator to the building's roof. It is a lovely space, set up for private parties and
offering dazzling views. The best view is to the south, where
the U.S. Capitol building gleams in artificial light. Only a couple of blocks away, it looks close enough to touch.

"I never knew my great uncle," Bill says, up on the roof.
"But I come up here and I remember the stories my dad tells
me about how he comes to Chicago, how he makes a success,
lives that American dream. I am named after him and so I
have always felt his shadow and I think it has instilled in all
of us kids the notion that hard work will bring success. Look
at my dad, look at what he did after taking over the tavern.
How can we not be proud of that? How can we not want to
continue this amazing story? It's not a burden, it's a joy. I like
to think my great uncle would be very happy about the Billy
Goat being in Washington. I think he would love this view."

THE AMERICAN
DREAM

Sam went back to Greece to find the love of his life.
He married Irene Dariotis in Chicago in November 1974.

Sam, shortly after
he arrived in
Chicago to work
for his uncle.

Sam's mother Theofana died an hour after his birth.

Two cowpokes: Roy Rogers and Billy.

Bill Veeck was one of Billy's great and most playful pals.

Sam ogles the 1974 World Series rings of Oakland A's shortstop Bert Campaneris (left) and team owner Charlie Finley.

Sam and Irene with Dave Condon (sans cigar) and his son David, who would work for a time at the tavern.

Sam with his father, Anthanasios, who worked for a while at the Hubbard Street tavern and whom every one called Tom.

Sam and Cubs broadcaster Jack Brickhouse.

Sam with Mike Royko, who was "more than a brother."

Dan Aykroyd and the late John Belushi autographed this *Blues Brothers* photo on one of their visits to the tavern.

Sam and Mayor Richard M. Daley, a White Sox fan.

Bill Murray has been a Billy Goat regular for decades.

Sarah Purcell of the TV show *Real People*, enjoying her visit with Sam and Bill Charuchas.

President George Bush stopped in to meet some regulars in 1991 but Mike Royko famously refused to make an appearance.

President Bill Clinton gets a new T-shirt after visiting Sam at the Billy Goat's oasis at Taste of Chicago.

Hillary Clinton stops in to visit with some of the Sianis family.

Famous enough for billboards: Sam poses with a massive wall side
promotion for the Illinois Lottery.

On Halloween, Sam sits with the carved pumpkin faces of Mike
and Billy.

Bill Sianis does not remember the first time his father took him to the Billy Goat but remembers a childhood "surrounded by goats . . . stuffed goat dolls at home. I think they were gifts from my father's friends. And when we would go to Greece we were always playing in the fields with goats and some sheep."

As for his first visit to the family business: "I can't remember, but there is a picture of me pulling one of the beer machines. I must have been about one."

And before that is the announcement of Bill's birth in Bob Herguth's January 21, 1975, column in the *Daily News*: "It's a first child for Sam and Irene Sianis . . . He weighs almost nine pounds and he's 21 inches long . . . His name? Billy Goat Jr. He'll be fixing hamburgers at the grill soon."

He and his brother, Tom, who is one year younger, "would come here Sundays after church and when we were real little would be locked into my dad's office. And sometimes we were allowed to sit at a table in the corner. The waiters would keep a close eye on us, and we would sit at that table and draw on paper with crayons. It was like a second home and I think he had us with him because he wanted to be with his kids," says Bill.

Later, he put the kids to work. "We were making cokes and helping the guys running the grill," he says. "On Saturdays he would drop us off at Greek school at St. Basil's and then come pick us up, and we would work with him until about seven and then go home. When we were 13, 14, we started working the grill."

Bill goes to the Illinois Institute of Technology to study architecture. He wants to build buildings, but he now helps run the business with his dad.

Tom now works as a state's attorney, but you will find him working the grill on most weekends and some nights. "Attorney by day, cook on weekends," he says.

"It has been amazing to watch these kids grow up," says Jeff. "They could be, maybe even should be, spoiled. But they are anything but. Sam exalts family."

There are other, younger brothers: Paul, an accountant, and Ted, a graphic artist, and they too followed in the Saturday Greek school–Billy Goat path as Bill and Tom. You will often find them working at and helping run the many Billy Goats.

And the last of Sam's and Irene's children are twin girls, Jennifer and Patty, pretty and lively, a physical therapist and a teacher. They work the busy Billy Goat booth every summer at Taste of Chicago.

Some Sundays, shortly after the Billy Goat opens at 11 A.M., you will see Irene and maybe one of the girls having breakfast at a table. Sam makes their food and then cooks for himself. He takes a hunk of garlic, as big as an infant's first, cracks it hard on the counter at the grill, peels it, and then slaps the cloves on the grill. He sprinkles olive oil on them, and, as the garlic sizzles, he cracks a couple of eggs and lets the whites fall to the griddle. A couple of seconds later, a quick maneuver with a spatula lifts the eggs and garlic, and he deposits them on a slice of rye bread. For lunch, he usually has a salad, and for dinner at home, maybe some chicken. He watches his diet, his health. But he will often eat a hamburger. "I'm not worried about getting fat," he says. "My hamburgers are lean and pure."

One day when he is sitting with filmmaker George Motz, Sam says this, pointing to his head: "I always tell my kids, you go to school. You get something in here. You get something in here and you can do anything. You can go into business 'cause any time you got something in here, nobody's ever going to be able to take it away from you. You can go into business and lose, but up in here [he taps his fingers to his head again] nobody can take it away."

Motz puts what Sam says in his movie *Hamburger America*. What he doesn't put in is what he tells me later: "What Sam said, the way he articulates that sense of family, that is the essence of the American dream."

A Chicago Tavern

When he arrives in Chicago in 1990 from his native Morocco, 23-year-old Bouchaib Khribech is planning to stay with a friend of a friend. But when that person fails to show up to meet his plane at O'Hare, the young man spends his first days in town nervously sleeping on the "L" and camping out in a park. Ten days in town and he finally has a job, busing tables at the Billy Goat. He becomes an ebullient presence, his English ever-improving as he takes the nickname Bouch, waits tables, tends bar, and grills burgers.

"He is a good worker," says Sam, offering the highest praise he has. Bouch's bright smile and radiant personality endear him to the tavern's crowd. Many become close friends. He is mentioned in many stories, and when he becomes an American citizen in 2000, he is celebrated in same-day columns by the *Tribune*'s John Kass and the *Sun-Times*' Mark Brown, a rare newsprint exacta usually reserved for crooked politicians.

This does not ruin Bouch. Neither does meeting former presidents Clinton and Bush and other celebrities who drop by for a burger and a photo opportunity. Bouch sends copies of the Christmas cards he gets from the Clintons and the photo of himself and Bush I to the King of Morocco, who is so impressed that he invites Bouch's mom for a visit to his palace.

Mom comes to Chicago, as does Bouch's sister Meryem and brother, Tarik. Tarik follows in Bouch's Billy Goat footsteps, as does another brother, Marouane, before him. The entire family is involved in the launch of Bouch's new business venture, Marrakech ExpressO on Damen Avenue.

Bouch works seven days a week at the Goat, always has, and plans to continue to do so. "It will be hard," he says, "but my family will help, and I like hard work. It is like a dream. When I first come here I sleep in the park four blocks away. Now I have this. It will be hard, but I know I can do it. I know life is about challenge."

At the end of the 2005 season, with fans filling the Billy Goats to watch the Chicago White Sox win their first World Series since 1917, the Cubs Curse is invoked by sportswriters across the country.

Later in the year Cubs general manager, Jim Hendry, tells reporter Carrie Muskat, "We're coming off a year we didn't expect. It doesn't feel good and [we] have to make us better for '06."

The only Billy Goat to ever fail is one that opens at 3516 N. Clark Street in 2004. It is only one block from Wrigley Field, and though it does well during the season, it does not do well when the Cubs are not at home. In less than two years it closes. "Maybe it is because the Cubs, they want to get back at my uncle because of the curse," says Sam, philosophically.

"It doesn't make me mad. I really would like to see the Cubs win. But I look at this year, and I think the curse is alive."

Shortly after 10 A.M. on the day after Halloween, two familiar faces show up at the Billy Goat. Mike and Billy are carried in by Clem Jaskot, who owns a place called Phyllis' Musical Inn on west Division Street. For the last couple of years Phyllis' is the setting for an extraordinary scene, as a couple dozen people gather to carve pumpkins according to the intricate designs created by a man named Craig Perry, who has been a pumpkin carver for nearly 20 years. The faces are of famous people, and they are displayed in Millennium Park, and are so recognizable and realistic that people gasp. Jaskot knows Jeff and he knows Sam, and so he has the carvers make the pumpkins of Billy and Mike as special gifts.

"Perpetual Halloween" the old place on Madison Street is called, and remembering or not, on this day, Sam hugs the Mike and Billy pumpkins as if they were living people and says, "It is almost like having them back to life."

The pumpkins, Mike and Billy, sit side by side through the day and into the night, amazing visitors and regulars and a family from California. Finally, the place is empty and Sam says, "Goodnight," to Mike and Billy.

In a few hours, Spiros will open the doors and start another tavern day. John and Bill will be in early for coffee, later for drinks, and who knows who else will open the door and walk down the stairs.

Right now, it is late and I am walking alone along the empty sidewalk, and Sam is in his car headed home, and at the Billy Goat the lights are out, chairs sit upside down on tables, the floor is clean, the doors are locked, and the place is as quiet as it is possible for a good tavern to be.

Acknowledgments

You would not be holding this book in your hands if Sam and Bill Sianis had not asked me one afternoon sitting around a table at the tavern, "Would you write a book about the Billy Goat?" I told them that if they wanted a book strictly for the tourist crowd we could slap it together in about 30 minutes: a lot of pictures, a few Mike Royko columns, some curse and *Saturday Night Live* stories.

But Sam said, "No, I want the real story for the tourists and everybody else too," and he then did everything in his considerable power to make it happen, correcting some longstanding errors in the historic record and offering honest and often heartfelt answers to every question I asked him. Bill guided the project with precision and patience and the rest of this remarkable family—wife and mother Irene, sons Tom, Paul, and Ted, and the twin daughters Jennifer and Patty—were generous with their time. But, then, that's the way they have always been.

Sharon Woodhouse, who single handedly launched Lake Claremont Press more than a decade ago and has since filled our collective bookshelf with fine Chicago books we might not otherwise have had, was enthusiastic, creative, and understanding from the outset. She gives publishers a good name. She also provided me with a remarkable group of collaborators in editor Bruce Clorfene, designer Charisse Antonopoulos, cover designer Tim Kocher, copywriter Jean Kozlowski, and that jack of many trades, Elizabeth Daniel. George Motz, a great filmmaker and a profound burger-thinker, offered the book's striking cover photo. The work of photographer Charles Osgood, my longtime collaborator on the "Sidewalks" columns in the *Chicago Tribune* magazine and great friend, graces many of these pages.

So many of the people who have worked and continue to work at the Billy Goats and to drink and eat and talk there provided not only a deeper understanding of the place but have offered years of friendship in exchange for nothing. Some are mentioned in the book. Others are not. You all share in this story.

Reading the work of all the writers who have, with varying degrees of literary license, told the story of the tavern through the years, reminded me why I got in this business in the first place. There were once poets working for newspapers.

A Chicago Tavern

John Cruickshank, publisher of the *Chicago Sun-Times*, graciously allowed my brother Mark Kogan to do some digging in that paper's "morgue." He came back with gold.

The *Chicago Tribune*, which gives me a place to work and where some of the words in this book first appeared, is filled with friends who helped in various ways, so thanks Rick Pearson, Mike Zajakowski, David Syrek, Joe Darrow, Jim Kirk, David Greising, and Maury Possley.

And thanks to all those *Chicago Daily News* alums who shared their stories; Judy Royko, who dug deep enough for tears to share a memory; Mike and Tim and Reilly and all the others who shared their nights and dreams and fears before checking out; Colleen and Fiona for being there; and the Cubs for being the Cubs.

LAKE CLAREMONT PRESS

Founded in 1994, Lake Claremont Press specializes in books on the Chicago area and its history, focusing on preserving the city's past, exploring its present environment, and cultivating a strong sense of place for the future. Visit us on the Web at www.lakeclaremont.com

Booklist

A Cook's Guide to Chicago: Where to Find Everything You Need and Lots of Things You Didn't Know You Did, 2nd Edition

The Politics of Place: A History of Zoning in Chicago

Wrigley Field's Last World Series: The Wartime Chicago Cubs and the Pennant of 1945

The Golden Age of Chicago Children's Television

Chicago's Midway Airport: The First Seventy-Five Years

The Hoofs & Guns of the Storm: Chicago's Civil War Connections

Great Chicago Fires: Historic Blazes That Shaped a City

The Firefighter's Best Friend: Lives and Legends of Chicago Firehouse Dogs

Graveyards of Chicago: The People, History, Art, and Lore of Cook County Cemeteries

Chicago Haunts: Ghostlore of the Windy City

More Chicago Haunts: Scenes from Myth and Memory

Muldoon: A True Chicago Ghost Story: Tales of a Forgotten Rectory

Creepy Chicago (for kids 8 - 12)

Literary Chicago: A Book Lover's Tour of the Windy City

A Field Guide to Gay & Lesbian Chicago

A Native's Guide to Chicago, 4th Edition

A Native's Guide to Northwest Indiana

Award-winners

Finding Your Chicago Ancestors: A Beginner's Guide to Family History in the City and Cook County

The Streets & San Man's Guide to Chicago Eats

The Chicago River: A Natural and Unnatural History

Near West Side Stories: Struggles for Community in Chicago's Maxwell Street Neighborhood

Hollywood on Lake Michigan: 100 Years of Chicago and the Movies

Coming in 2006

Today's Chicago Blues

For Members Only: A History and Guide to Chicago's Oldest Private Clubs

From Lumber Hookers to the Hooligan Fleet: A Treasury of Chicago Maritime History

Coming in 2007

On the Job: Behind the Stars of the Chicago Police Department

Chicago TV Horror Movie Shows: From Shock Theater to Svengoolie

"The Next Big Thing" — The Uncensored Story of Chicago Rock's Explosions and Implosions in the 1990s

Rick Kogan is a Chicago newspaperman.

The Sianis Family owns and operates the Billy Goat taverns.